Felicity &
Barbara Pym

Harrison Solow

Published by Cinnamon Press
Meirion House,
Glan yr afon,
Tanygrisiau,
Blaenau Ffestiniog,
Gwynedd,
LL41 3SU.
www.cinnamonpress.com

The right of Yvonne Harrison Solow aka Harrison Solow to be
identified as the author of this work has been asserted by her in
accordance with the Copyright, Designs and Patent Act, 1988 as
© Harrison Solow, 2010
ISBN: 978-1-907090-11-0
British Library Cataloguing in Publication Data. A CIP record
for this book can be obtained from the British Library

Designed and typeset in Garamond by Cinnamon Press. Cover
design by Mike Fortune-Wood from original artwork 'Young
Female Studying' by Yuri Arcurs, agency: dreamstime.com.
Printed in Poland.

Cinnamon Press is represented in the UK by Inpress Ltd
www.inpressbooks.co.uk and in Wales by the Welsh Books
Council www.cllc.org.uk.

The publisher acknowledges the financial support of the Welsh
Books Council.

Contents

Author's Preface

The idea for this book can be traced to an incident that took place in my undergraduate astronomy class at university many years ago.

The lecturer began with the Big Bang, a theory to which, despite extensive examination, I have never quite warmed. His opening statement to us was that '*before there was anything*, there were particles floating around in the universe. I raised my hand and when called upon, asked (logically, I thought then), 'What universe? If there was nothing, then there was nothing. I don't understand.'

Accordingly, he revised his statement to say that there *were* sub-atomic particles in existence, to which I again asked, politely, 'Where did they come from?' His answer was, 'Miss Cooper, you are an English major—why are you in this class?' I replied that I was in university *to learn* [I was very young] and therefore was truly interested to know where these particles came from.

Whereupon he walked to the door, opened it, pointed down the corridor and said frostily, 'This is an Astronomy class. We begin with the Big Bang. If you want to know where the particles came from, the Theology Department is down the hall, and the Philosophy Department is upstairs.'

Until that moment, it had not been my understanding, nor my experience, meagre as it was, that astronomy, philosophy, theology and literature could be unrelated. And, as the performance of the Astronomy professor did not convince me otherwise, I have persisted in the belief that they are not. It still seems to me that none of the traditional components of the trivium or quadrivium is so far removed from another, or from the other arts, that the effort to understand one does not benefit all.

And I am still convinced that enquiry is the passport to genuine understanding.

I have found in my own education that a jumble of seemingly unrelated facts or principles can coalesce into a magnificently unified microcosm, wherein all components balance beautifully, harmoniously and usefully with the application of appreciation to knowledge. What I have not found is that most universities support this unification theory, although some faculty members do reward it at times, when manifested in an individual student's performance.

'Felicity' is the silent student in this short volume of correspondence. The name, however, represents neither a particular person, nor the synonym for joy. Rather, it is the name of a disposition that I have encountered repeatedly in my younger students (and far too often for comfort in my older students) a sensibility that can best be described as a 'happy disregard' of centuries of interrelated scholarship intrinsic to a liberal arts education. This disregard extends to the tools one needs in order to benefit from the study of any subject, the chief of which is the rigorous employment of reason, infused with enough imagination to see the subject as alive and enough appreciation to see it as relevant.

Such a blithe preoccupation with the present tends to inculcate a dismissive attitude to all that is not immediately discernible as being personally valuable. This is often curable, of course. Time works its usual transformation. But how much time is wasted in the intervening years—the years wherein a Felicity Halper may wear make-up in shades called Bruise and Slime, and expect not to be judged; yet herself disregard the education, emotion and experience of a Barbara Pym simply because she may be judged, from this dubious perspective, as outmoded.

Now, Barbara Pym's work is hardly at the heart of a liberal education. But because she is such an antithesis to the prevailing attitude; because her work has been undervalued; and because, in the end, my own research includes intertextuality, interdisciplinarity and the liberal arts, I have chosen to address these matters by way of Barbara Pym.

This is not a work of literary criticism—it is not a work of literary theory. It is an attempt to illustrate the value of *appreciation* in the study of literature by reading it in context, not merely in the context of the author, but in the context of the civilisation of literature itself. We do not read, after all, as a species, in order that we may deconstruct and dissect. People buy books and borrow books from libraries because they like them. They read, re-read, recommend, learn from, incorporate values from, live by, study and take to bed at night, books they like; books they appreciate; books they find meaningful. Appreciation is not perhaps what the university requests of its students today. But it is what writers (who are, after all, the sole source upon which the existence of English departments depend) deserve.

And though there is much to bemoan about universities today, I wish to acknowledge those who, among my many academic colleagues are true scholars, admirable teachers, highly educated men and women from whose erudition, congeniality, friendship, good company, and common sense (and tutelage when I was Felicity's age) I have truly benefitted. I know how hard they work and how long. I know how much they care about their students, their subjects and their departments. This is not about them or any specific university out of the many I have attended or at which I lectured or taught. Most references to universities in this work are to a conglomerate, like the character of Felicity. They are often metaphorical institutions.

There are no chapters in this 'collection of letters,' only broadly defined sections. The premise that all subjects are interrelated is best served by eliminating sharp divisions.

Barbara Pym's novels are quoted often throughout the text and the following abbreviations have been used:

Some Tame Gazelle: STG
Excellent Women: EW
Jane and Prudence: JP
Less Than Angels: LTA
A Glass of Blessings: GB
No Fond Return of Love: NFR
Quartet in Autumn: QA

The Sweet Dove Died: SDD
A Few Green Leaves: FGL
An Unsuitable Attachment: UA
Crampton Hodnet: CH
An Academic Question: AQ

This work is both fiction and non-fiction. It will be up to the reader, if it matters, to determine which is which.

Harrison Solow
Malibu, California
1997- 2010

Introduction

Harrison Solow is a writer of experience at least as diverse as that of her principal voice in this unusual, charming and astringent piece of writing which some will read as an epistolary novel (no adjectival form of the term 'e-mail' having yet been generated), some as both a practical and philosophical introduction to, and summing-up of, the nature and uses of literature and its discussion — and others as a delightfully readable and comic drama of the generations, of the cantankerous yet worldly-wise tutor and the idealistic yet impatient young American student trying to set up lines of communication about the (highly) English novelist Barbara Pym -- not to mention the strange pathways that lie between the cradle and the grave, linking even Tunbridge Wells, a West Wales butcher and Hollywood.

Harrison Solow's creation Mallory Cooper, while constantly negotiating a constellation of identities that range between the American, the Catholic, the Jewish, the English and the Welsh has, notwithstanding, yet to find the fence on which she might be willing to sit. This is a book of strong opinions, valiant, forthright and elegant, laid out in defiance of yea-sayers, bet-hedgers, academic bureaucrats and bureaucratic academics. It will infuriate as well as stimulate (as Mallory Cooper, who is not short of self-knowledge, well knows), prompt both wry and outright laughter and stir deeper reflections. It should be mandatory reading for all undergraduate students of English Literature; no American students of English Literature should be allowed to set foot upon campus without having proved that they have read it (as well as answering a brief catechism on the subject of afternoon tea, high tea, dinner, supper and lunch — and explaining to Mallory Cooper's satisfaction the significance of 'dowdiness' within a British context). They will be the more likely to obtain a degree if they do. After all, their tutors will certainly read it.

And if there emerges from all this a valuable reader's guide to Barbara Pym (and there does), it is as a by-product of what is a fluent testimony and exploration of writing, reading, the significance of value, the rigours of understanding and judgement, and the fact that it is adult to realise that there are no short-cuts to scholarship. For Barbara Pym's novels also just happen to be the subject of that first term-paper that Felicity the new student must write, a stalking-horse for the whole host of literary, cultural, philosophical and spiritual issues that restlessly inhabit Mallory Cooper (and which – one should stress -- do not specifically demand of the reader any prior knowledge of Pym to appreciate and enjoy).

Peter Miles,
Emeritus Fellow of the English Association.

Foreword

Of all the books that have been written about Barbara (and how she would have smiled at some of them) this is the one with which I am most in sympathy.

Original, controversial, academic, readable, serious, light-hearted, sensible, charming – there is no end to the words that could be applied to *Felicity and Barbara Pym*. The framework, letters to a new student of English Literature, allows Harrison Solow to range widely over many topics and, in the process of examining the work of one author in detail, take her readers on a leisurely ramble though English literature during which she shares with them the treasures of a cultured mind.

The underlying premise of this splendid book is the importance of the *appreciation* of literature – something that has too often been mislaid along the way in critical exploration. The choice of Barbara Pym, by no means a mainstream author and one very much of her period, may be surprising but, as we discover, she is an eminently satisfactory subject for the author's sympathetic analysis and her invaluable advice about considering a writer in his or her own particular setting, as well as the universal qualities in Barbara Pym's work that go beyond time and fashion, as Philip Larkin noted so perceptively.

Students and tutors and, indeed, everyone who has ever found enjoyment in reading, will be grateful for this delightful work. I loved it and I can say with confidence that Barbara would have loved it too.

Hazel Holt
February 19, 2010

for Baker, Canon and Brooke

Felicity

December 19, 2 _____

Dear Felicity,

How happy you are in your circumstance, as well as your name! I can think of few happier moments than the unblemished beginning of a new academic semester, particularly at such a respectable institution as Yarmouth. (Although I always think it such a pity that it fell to co-education — I believe we must allow our brothers to enjoy the gender peace that we claim at Smith, Mills, Wellesley, etc.) Still, it is a good thing for you, and I wish you great satisfaction.

And no, I don't think it that Whitley would have been a better choice than Yarmouth — though not having met you yet, I feel hesitant in expressing an opinion which, to be of any use, must be dependent on some acquaintance with your own goals, desires, preferences. But Yarmouth has two advantages. One, it used to be a men's college, therefore people will think you cleverer for having attended it than Whitley which tends to be regarded as a finishing school in some, unenlightened it is true, circles — but then how often our futures are made or at least affected by the unenlightened, and; two, it is in New England.

Now that I have had my first letter from you, I think this 'tutoring by email' is a good idea. I had the usual doubts when Dr. Hall suggested it, but it has turned out to be one of his many good ideas, I feel. He has been a dear friend for many years, and I am sure an excellent advisor to you. His illness is a daily sorrow to me, the only good consequence of which is that I have inherited his tutelage of you, which will be a pleasure. I am delighted that he is taking this semester off.

Your studies sound enviable. I feel a great longing at times to escape from 'the industry' as it is called in LA (as if there were only one) and be back among the eucalyptus trees and fresh, perhaps rarefied, air at Mills College, teaching and being taught. Of course, my wish is for a past, not a present state of academic life and like all nostalgia, a mere indulgence. And thus, short-lived.

Speaking of which, to answer your question, yes, I have heard Mills College called 'the Vassar of the West,' although I hardly know why, since it predates Vassar by nine years (1852 as opposed to 1861) and by rights should claim precedence in the comparison; Vassar being the 'Mills of the East' so to speak. I can only imagine that it is that same 'centre of the universe' mentality, oddly characteristic of academia, which also prompts Southern Californians to speak of 'the industry,' meaning of course the entertainment industry, when there are dozens of flourishing occupations and businesses in this corner of the world.

I pray you do not adopt such a mentality after four years in an Ivy, (with its strangely appropriate connotations of creeping tendrils, tenacity and poison) but of course you will. If, after only a few pages of *Some Tame Gazelle*, you have made an authoritative pronouncement on the 'irrelevance of the genre' I hold out little hope that you will be spared such an attitude about other areas you have not yet experienced which fall under your scrutiny. But no matter. You will be cured. As I was. As we all were — all of us with media-bright, unopposed, well-nurtured American childhoods. But back to your first question.

You must recall, if not from history then at least from all those childhood books you mentioned, that the East (north and south) was regarded as the only real centre of civilisation in the middle of the last century. Anything west of the Mississippi was the wilderness — Indians, floods, locusts, lumberjacks, etc. I have here an amusing history book written in the thirties, speaking of 'savages' and the

'Colt's six shooter that ruled the mining towns' whereas in the East — well, you have read Henry James.

But do you remember five-year-old Laura Ingalls in *The Little House in the Big Woods* being so proud of Ma because she was from the East and had such a fine dress with blackberry shaped buttons that was made by an *eastern* dressmaker? And our Western films, hundreds of them with proper, ladylike, *eastern* schoolmarms whom everyone seemed to regard with unusual deference. With reason, usually. Have you ever seen High Noon? That sort of mentality. Not that it matters for our purposes, but it is perhaps the reason for the respective positions of the colleges in the metaphor (or metonym, really). And yet, Vassar seems to be co-ed now, while five of the remaining Six Sisters (alas — Radcliffe is no more) remain as they were, as does Mills, which detracts somewhat from the accuracy of the comparison, don't you think?

In any case, the real reason for my letter is to answer your cry for help in the matter of your upcoming Barbara Pym seminar. I will answer you with two comments. One, to reassure you, yes I do know something about Barbara Pym. Indeed she is one of my most valued friends, as are the other inhabitants of my bedside bookshelves; and two, I cannot believe what I read in your letter: 'Nothing ever happens in Barbara Pym's novels.' Are we talking about the same Pym? Or have we somehow strayed into that bizarre Monty Python sketch about Grate Expectations by that well known Dutch author, Charles Dikkens?' Are you speaking of some other author, named, perhaps, Pim?

Truly, Felicity, I don't know how to respond to that. I think I will take a little time and write to you in the next day or so with my comments. In the meantime, please read — no — absorb *Some Tame Gazelle*. You say you have four weeks before Winter Semester begins, and six novels to read before your first class. Believe me, you will have few more pleasant tasks in your life, and yes, I will see to it that you are well prepared.

You have not told me which six novels you are required to read. I suggest you read the following ten, in the order they were published:

Some Tame Gazelle 1950 (begun in 1933)
Excellent Women 1952
Jane and Prudence 1953
Less Than Angels 1955
A Glass of Blessings 1958
No Fond Return of Love 1961
Quartet in Autumn 1977
The Sweet Dove Died 1978
A Few Green Leaves 1980
An Unsuitable Attachment (written 1963, published 1980 posthumously)

Please use the editions that Dr. Hall recommended. I will use the same ones, as it is best that in our discussions, you and I are on the same page — so to speak.

Yours,
Mallory Cooper

December 22, 2____

Dear Felicity,

If you were going to teach English to foreign students who had never been in this country and never known an American, what would you choose as suitable background reading? Someday I will tell you what I chose and would continue to choose if I were still in that field, but for you, who are in somewhat of the same position as those students with respect to Miss Pym's England, I offer a reading list in order to help you digest the richness of *Some Tame Gazelle*. Of course, I know that you will not get through a tenth of these, nor perhaps are all necessary, but any that you can manage will help. The following are all available in Penguin paperback:

Lark Rise to Candleford, by Flora Thompson (Do *not* watch the BBC production. Read the book.)
English Eccentrics, by Edith Sitwell
The English by J.B. Priestley
Victoria's Heyday, by J. B. Priestley

Anything by Somerset Maugham, Margaret Drabble, Iris Murdoch, and A.S. Byatt, who is, as you may know, Margaret Drabble's sister. I recommend (your professors will no doubt sneer at this), a few early books by Miss Read (whose real name is Dora Saint). Her books are light-hearted accounts of village life in the 50s, 60s, 70s and 80s and although not regarded as the same calibre as the understated Miss Pym's work, they are nonetheless a fine introduction into a social structure, era, vocabulary and culture far different from your own.

I once had a correspondence with her — she sent me a fine recipe for a delicious and indigestible lardy cake — and we spoke of some of the differences between 'lofty academia' and 'real life' as I recall, although I happen to be one who thinks real life can be lived anywhere — even in a university. We did disagree on this point. Though after my recent visiting lectureship in a university in Great Britain, I do see her point.

I prefer the wide curiosity, broader curriculum, longer program and habit of innovation of American universities (of my experience of course), which is something we have in common, Felicity. We just draw the line of academic idealism in different places. Which means that, in my ideal world all undergraduate liberal arts programs would be clones of the one at St John's College and I'd save the broader curriculum for graduate school. Have a look at their website: www.stjohnscollege.edu/ and click on their admissions videos. This is what an education is. This is what to watch when one despairs of the human race. This is what I spent a lot of time watching in the days before I made the decision to resign from my last university. This is what I watch for sheer pleasure.

Well. In any case, as we are clearly not at St. John's, see if you can also pick up Elizabeth Goudge's *Damerhosebay Trilogy* and some pre and post war novels by D.E. Stevenson. These books are not considered great literature or even literature at all by most, including me, but they are stories, some of them excellent stories (the same stories from which, in other hands, literature grows and takes shape) and solid reflections of the same culture and era (in which these authors lived and about which they wrote) as Barbara Pym. I think you will find great (and many) similarities of tone, attitude, cultural and moral values, habits, customs, foods, assumptions, rituals, language, class, education and society between these illuminating tales and those works that are considered literature by people who think they know about such things – as well as by the people who do.

They will not have Miss Pym's delicate verbal economy, or her literary grace, but they will have her concerns. We are just beginning to create a picture of Pym's world so to speak, so bear with me. We will get to the critics later.

A few old issues of Punch would be enormous assets if you can get hold of them. You may or may not know about this weekly British humour magazine. From 1841 to 1992, it was a prominent publication. It was named after Mr. Punch of Punch and Judy fame, and was highly regarded by the well-educated public, chiefly for its brilliant, incisive satirical articles on political and social issues of the day, as well as its biting and witty cartoons of the same subjects. Your own favourite Winnie-the-Pooh author, A.A. Milne, was a regular contributor. Which reminds me, don't neglect children's books as an infinitely valuable source of information about a culture. You can tell a lot about a nation by reading what it writes for its own children. Along that line try Noel Streatfield, Milne of course, E. Nesbit, C. S. Lewis, and of course P.L. Travers — think of Mary Poppin's values!

It may seem unnecessary, but it is not. There is an unconscious cultural code in these books that upholds certain standards, believes in certain values, and incorporates certain attitudes and prejudices of the time — sometimes blatant, more often than not extremely subtle. They teach the young the subtext of their language — they instil that almost universal sense of superiority, however misguided, that graces — or infects — Albion's fair shore. They create (or did, in the era that we are examining) Englishness:

> Little Indian, Sioux or Crow
> Little Frosty Eskimo
> Little Turk or Japanee
> O! Don't you wish that you were me?

You have seen the scarlet trees
And the lions over seas
You have eaten ostrich eggs
And turned the turtles off their legs

Such a life is very fine
But it's not so nice as mine
You must often as you trod
Wearied not to be abroad

You have curious things to eat
I am fed on proper meat
You must dwell beyond the foam
But I am safe and live at home

Little Indian, Sioux or Crow
Little Frosty Eskimo
Little Turk or Japanee
O! Don't you wish that you were me?
    (Robert Louis Stevenson A *Child's Garden of Verses*)

Now, apart from the appalling xenophobia, this could be regarded simply as any well-fed, secure and happy child's view of the world, and it does have a certain universal innocent and myopic charm, but in this case it also represents an attitude of semi-sweet smugness that you will find over and over in English literature. That tone is apparent in one of the first publications written specifically for children, (possibly by Oliver Goldsmith) *The History of Little Goody Two-Shoes*. It was published by bookseller John Newbery, in (approximately) 1765. Newbery, you will recall, is the enlightened man in whose honour the Newbery medal for excellence in children's literature was established in 1921. He was the first English bookseller/publisher to regard children as a separate reader market.

There are earlier works. Pride of place probably goes to Mary Cooper's *Tommy Thumb's Pretty Song Book*, the earliest known collection of nursery rhymes, published in 1744. This was quickly followed by the now more familiar *Mother Goose's Melody* in 1760.

For the next hundred years or so, nothing of note was produced for children except 'moral tales', rather gruesome accounts of the dire consequences of disobedience, pride, gluttony, etc. The children featured in these stories nearly always died (or at least were horribly disfigured) in the wayward pursuit of their own (mostly innocuous) desires. A kind of instant Kiddie Karma imposed by a benevolent Supreme Being. ('God is Love' as they say.) Dickens is particularly adroit at portraying this repugnant hypocrisy. As is Charlotte Bronte's *Jane Eyre*, which you will read if you haven't already. Of course you must have. It is still a standard requirement in secondary schools today, isn't it?

Around 1860, a truly significant children's literature began to take shape. England initiated a body of work that endures to this day — work that was read by Barbara Pym, and almost certainly read (or seen in Disney form) by you. *Alice in Wonderland* (Lewis Carroll, 1865) for example. So you see, Felicity, were you and Miss Pym ever to have met, you would have had a good deal to say to each other, at least on one subject. Though I suspect there may be others.

'England could be reconstructed entirely from its children's books,' said Paul Hazard in his *Books, Children and Men*, and I think it is true. You will find echoes of Robert Louis Stevenson in *Some Tame Gazelle*:

> There appeared in rapid succession several pictures of handsome natives dressed in bunches of leaves and garlands of flowers. Some members of the audience were inclined to giggle at these but the bishop hastily

explained that the pictures were of the natives as they used to be.

'We have since introduced a form of European dress which is far more in keeping with Christian ideas of morality,' he said. (STG pg. 177)

(Don't you wish that you were me…)

But of course, you haven't reached that point in the novel, have you? And I was recommending background material to you — I seem to have strayed. Well, H.V. Morton's *In Search of England* will certainly help. Anthony Trollope's oeuvre (though that is asking a bit much) would give breadth to Pym's origins, although you may prefer his literary and literal descendent, Joanna's work, which would also help you to put together a cultural pattern of Miss Pym's environment, albeit in a slimmer realm. George Orwell's incisive *The Lion and the Unicorn* is a gem, and blessedly short.

I would recommend Anita Brookner — but that is really a reversal — Pym will help you understand her, or at least a certain something in her exquisite work that she herself seems not to understand, perhaps because she is lacking that insularity which makes the English, English, or more likely, because her autobiographical heroines struggle incessantly, never in balance, 'between two worlds, one dead, the other powerless to be born.'

I just spent a few minutes looking up the origin of that quotation, which sprang unbidden from my mind — I knew it was Matthew Arnold, but had forgotten from which poem. It is from 'Stanzas from the Grande Chartreuse.' Unlike Pym's heroines, I usually cannot quote content, author and source. And 'a few minutes' because I chose to refer to my books and not the Internet on this occasion.

Much more satisfying — a reward earned rather than the result of digital effluvia too freely dispensed, too effortlessly gained.

But they do raise a point — these unbidden quotations. They are really part of the answer to two of the questions you have asked me — why read Literature at all, and why Pym in particular. But I do not think we are ready to embark upon answers yet. Not, quite, yet.

And now 'I must away' as Shakespeare was wont to say, to prepare my lecture for the American Association for the Advancement of Science on 'The Science in Science Fiction'. Just another path along which those with English degrees may wander, and be paid for the journey. (Research skills intact and a huge body of work digested, of course.)

Science fiction, once relegated to that nebulous category of 'other' which includes Romance and Westerns, is now considered a legitimate genre and, as such, is permissible to address in educated circles. Whether it is valuable as a body of literature or not is another matter. But I foresee another digression. We shall continue tomorrow.

Best —

Mallory Cooper

PS You must, you must, read Anita Brookner, quite probably the best, and certainly one of the three best, English (fiction and nonfiction) writers living today.

December 23, 2_____

Dear Felicity,

Yes, I am against missionaries. Imagine barging into someone else's country and changing their clothes — re-dressing them! And only because you find their habiliment discomfiting — a situation easily avoided by not invading their culture in the first place. What chutzpah. It is inconceivable that you or I would allow emissaries from foreign lands to march into Cleveland or Boston or anywhere else in this nation and tell us what to wear and how to think. How can it possibly enter any sane person's head to do this to someone else? Good grief. And no I am not against foreign aid. They are quite, quite separate activities.

Speaking of clothes and cultures, I am sending you by post, Jilly Cooper's irreverent book, *Class*, and lest after reading it, you feel amused and comfortably assured of our own American democratic society, I am including a book by Paul Fussell, also entitled *Class*. The former describes British society; the latter American. These may be among the most informative books on our list. They are not academic works, nor do they purport to be, but this does not mean that they are not useful or serious, however amusing. You will find that they make the same observations about society as the 20th century cultural critics acceptable to academia, as well as novelists whose literary status entitles them to cultural commentary without reproach, among whom are Forster, Huxley, Woolf, and Wilson.

I am assuming that you will be working on your Pym preparation through this unreasonably long Winter Break, and will examine this supplementary reading list and garner from it what you can in order to understand Miss Pym in her context, a little better.

You may therefore, want to explore the marvellous *Cider with Rosie* by Laurie Lee, and almost any memoir of any English contemporary of Barbara Pym (she was born June 2, 1913 and died in 1980). Pick one at random from the library — whether well or poorly written, there will be common cultural threads — and it is your task to discover what they are. Add to these at least some of the poets of whom Miss Pym's characters are fond — Coventry Patmore, Matthew Arnold, Tennyson, Pope, Milton, Goldsmith, Keats, Gray, Marvell, Donne, Rossetti, et al, and you will begin to gain some foothold on the uncertain terrain of the world you are entering. And it is a different world — do not make the mistake of assuming that because we appear to understand our 'common language' that we understand each other. Our languages stopped being common in the 18th Century, which is why we still say 'dove' for the past tense of dive and 'gotten' instead of got, and use words like 'platter' for dish and phrases like 'I guess' as Chaucer and Shakespeare did and modern Britons don't. Have a look in the OED. Preferably the gargantuan two-volume version that my dear former father in law cherished, which came with a formidable magnifying glass and needed four burly countrymen to lift. He and I had a vigorous and pleasurable contretemps once about "dove" being the past tense of "dive" which he said it wasn't and then of course, resorting to the tome with a flourish of confidence, positively brandishing the magnifying glass at me like a weapon, found that it was. To be fair, it was about 20 entries down with *"N. Am Dialect"* after it.

And, by the way, when Chaucer was writing, the official language of England was French. In fact, if you ever come across that tiresome, puerile, pompous attitude towards the American language as I did when I first lived in England (don't you wish that you were me?), you would do well to remember that had the fledgling USA not chosen English as its operative language, no one in Britain would be speaking

English today.

In the early days of the Union, it was not a foregone conclusion that English would be our common language. Greek, Hebrew and French were seriously discussed as alternatives to the English that was beginning to dominate. With such a polyglot society as existed at the time, any language could have been chosen. And as the United States grew to super power status and the population far outnumbered that of England, whatever language the USA chose would have become the lingua franca for the world. Have a look at *The Story of English*, by Robert McCrum, William Cran and Robert MacNeil.

Moreover, we have been studying English Literature in universities longer than our British cousins. According to university historian Julian Lindsay, the Department of English at the University of Vermont was established in or about 1827 and was the first department of English literature in America. Harvard's English department was not created until 1876, and, in England, no Department of English existed until Oxford established the Merton Professorships of English Language and Literature in 1885.

Back to investigating cultures. You will notice that I have not asked you to read any critical political, sociological, literary, anthropological, or cultural history academic texts. This is not my mandate. I wish you to read literature. In addition to that (and we have not yet determined between us what 'that' is) I specifically wish you to read books and stories, tales and fictional accounts of England by contemporaries of Barbara Pym. Your academic teachers will advise you on critical and other texts. I want you to feel the vocabulary and the syntax and the concerns and the themes — the flavour and the manners and the foods and the tools of Barbara Pym's world. I want you to read the wartime recipes and learn the slang — to observe what was considered polite and politic, what values, customs, beliefs were assumed in various social circumstances. I want you to get a sense of how much church attendance mattered or did not — and why. I want you to know what a ration book was and what beauty meant and how grievous, how *grievous,* an infraction it was in that society to be sexually active before marriage. Or to be thought to be so. I want you to know what it meant to be part of a village and what it means to mend a pair of winter gloves. I want you to know the words that convey these things and how they do so. And, if you can, why. I want you to learn these things from the people who were there at the time and felt motivated or compelled to write about them. You will get the retrospective and the spin and the analysis and the conclusions of historians and critics from your assigned reading in your course. I want you to have more. Of course this is not to say that context and biographical details are sufficient to understand an author. Many writers transcend or are otherwise at variance with the times and cultures in which they live. But there is no way to discern that without knowing the context.

You will no doubt glean insights of your own and find texts to consult from your other Literature courses, particularly your Nineteenth Century British Novel class. (By which is meant "English Novel"—I doubt if there are Welsh novels on the syllabus) Your art history course, which I imagine you are richly enjoying, will also prove invaluable.

And now I have given you far too much to do — even selectively, but it will prove to be a gift indeed. It is richness and joy for days you cannot imagine yet. Perhaps it is too much to ask anyone under forty to read Barbara Pym. Like the Kabbalah, it requires a certain burning off of earlier, more raw perceptions — but then, here we are — you have a seminar for which to prepare and I have a pupil to prepare for it.

Now to the postscript in your last note. You say you would like to know something about me and ask what I do in Los Angeles. First of all, I do not live in LA. I live in

Malibu, which is roughly thirty miles from West LA, UCLA, Beverly Hills, as you know. I am a writer, as no doubt Dr. Hall has told you. I work at home in my office in a monastic sort of house that my husband and I treasure, overlooking the Pacific Ocean. I have been an English Professor at UC Berkeley, a visiting lecturer at several American and British universities, an Editor at a university press and other research institutions. I have been a professional writer for an enormous number of organizations and institutions and a speechwriter for various celebrities, among many other labels that a writer who must pay the rent will acquire in the course of her career. Now that, due to a certain measure of success in those worlds, I no longer have to pay rent or even a mortgage, I am simply writing books. Full-time. I also continue to write for the film industry in various ways, both peripherally and essentially in some respects, but that requires more information than is reasonable to ask me to dispense in this note. I am currently writing my fifth book — I have just finished the fourth — and I am editing a philosophy manuscript for academic publication. I'm beginning a sixth book (a novel this time) and preparing the first stages of a six-hour mini-series on the Jewish way of life for a Judeo-Christian organization for which I am an advocate.

I occasionally tutor other students — right now, a fourteen-year-old prodigy; I study Jewish philosophy with a very learned and exacting Rabbi and Cymreictod and Welsh spirituality with a very learned and exacting Jesuit. I study Welsh. I try to keep up my French. I have coffee with my writer friends. My husband and I host dinner parties in our house for intimate friends and in restaurants for business colleagues. I am, in short, a writer.

As such, I am happily and fortunately engaged in my customary dialectic with a dazzling array of minds of various persuasions — Jesuits, artists, lawyers, rabbis, novelists, designers, movie and television writers, producers, directors, costume designers, makeup artists, etc., astronauts, stockbrokers, science fiction writers, shopkeepers, musicians, Franciscans, poets, Buddhists, dancers, atheists, publicists, actors, taxi-drivers, Welsh teachers, businesspeople, chefs, children, New York playwrights, farmers, students, librarians, journalists, astrophysicists, scholars, novelists, Men and Women of (French, English and Welsh) Letters, family, politicians, and more.

Some of these descriptions overlap of course — a Jesuit who is a stunning Man of Letters, an astrophysicist who plays the violin like a star, etc. But most have a predominant identity. While this sounds somewhat fanciful, it is true. And with rare and shining exceptions, none of these people are university colleagues. They are friends of wide experience and compelling depth that I made by circumstance, by initiative, by curiosity, by work and by showing up. And that tells you very little about me. But you did ask what I do and this is some of it. It is also a partial answer to your question—'what can I do with an English degree?'

With all good thoughts,

Mallory Cooper

PS Yes, I do teach a university course on Anita Brookner from time to time — in conjunction with Barbara Pym. Dr. Brookner is an entirely different literary category – a much more profound writer morally and aesthetically than Miss Pym— a master (mistress) of her art. However, because so many people think that these authors are so similar, I feel obligated to teach a course which points out that they are not. The course description is attached.

Anita Brookner and Barbara Pym Syllabus:

The late twentieth century could as easily be defined by its conflicts—its clash of ideologies, its tempests, its lethal ideals as anything else. Not even the hermetic worlds of the decorous village spinster, or the shy London wife have remained entirely untouched.

In this course we explore two notable twentieth (in Brookner's case, also twenty-first) century English female novelists, whose serene and elegant depictions of human needs, loves, hates, fears, foibles, and resistance to the disruptive tide of change reflect both their own circumscribed societies and civilization at large.

Barbara Pym, hailed as a twentieth century Jane Austen, and Anita Brookner, also hailed as a twentieth century Jane Austen, have both perfected narrative art (Brookner to an exquisite level) in the fictional microcosms they created. They are often compared to each other and to the same literary progenitors as their work appears to be related — even interconnected — metaphorically, literally and logically.

In this course however, we claim that it is not, and more importantly we examine why. We investigate the hidden theme in the canon of both novelists, a theme that appears to be identical and yet somehow translates into contradictory definitions — the metaphysics of 'belonging' in the worlds of Barbara Pym, and of 'not belonging' in those of Brookner. Oddly both writers reach similar conclusions but not because they are alike. The tensions within and between the mainstream and marginal societies, the Anglican-Christian and Jewish ideologies (and their consequent moral preoccupations) from which these women respectively derive, form the focus of enquiry into these two novelists — two opposite arcs of a circle of uneasy thought.

These two female novelists of 20th Century England will be examined against the more robust and contemporary feminist prose of Margaret Drabble and A.S. Byatt whose works epitomise the evolving literary and cultural matrix from which they arise, and of whom it has not been said that any connection to Jane Austen is either visible or desirable.

The purpose of this course is threefold:

1. To provide an introduction to two exceptional contemporary female writers whose worlds both co-exist and collide;
2. To analyse 'perfected' writing – specifically how contrary ideologies in aesthetic narrative constructs find a common denominator; and
3. To examine, referentially, the heritage of English literature in which derivation, innovation, and application of perfected language to a 'very small piece of ivory' constitute and extend the literary tradition.

Upon successful completion of this course, students should be able to discern the roles of culture, perception, language and ideological tradition in literary works that both manifest and transcend the era in which they were written. They should also be able to recognise, define and demonstrate the word 'literature' and to discern levels within it. To this end, students will be required within the seminar to 'perfect' two texts of their own — one creative and the other critical.

December 24, 2_____

Dear Felicity,

So — you are going home today. I wish you a good journey and a rewarding visit with your family in Santa Barbara Thank you for your home email address, but are you certain you will be in a frame of mind to continue this correspondence during the next week? Thank you also for your very beautiful Christmas card — and to answer your question as to how I will spend Christmas, I do not know — happily, I hope.

Perhaps I will spend it with Christians, and see 'how they love one another.' (Tertullian. *Apologeticus* xxxix) By that I mean of course, that I am not a 'Christian' the way you appear to define it and therefore will not be celebrating in the way you describe, but will certainly be appreciative of the fleeting goodwill that pops up *en masse* each December.

And, lest I sound cynical, I do recall the transfixed awe of Christmas I experienced as a child, breathing in with every plume of incense, glory, hope, trust... It was and is astonishing — and I wish you the sweetest, simplest, most loving holiday season you can sustain.

But it is interesting how, in the kind, inclusive sending of a card, one makes a cultural assumption, as do, you will discover, Barbara Pym's characters. (Not everyone celebrates Christmas, Felicity.) You may have more in common with these men and women than you think. And less. But that is the discovery — that is the diversion and the substance of literature, and that is perhaps part of the answer you seek. I'd like to know, at the end of our study, with which character you resonate most. 'A Happy, Holy Christmas,' said Harriet reading from Father Plowman's card,' in *Some Tame Gazelle*.

The very same to you, Felicity.

MC

PS My husband and I are having Christmas dinner with the same dear friends who came to our house for the second night of Chanukah.

Silly Men

December 26, 2 _____

Dear Felicity,

Thank you for your email — I am glad that our correspondence seems to be of help. And you have finished *Some Tame Gazelle*. Now we begin.

Your notes aren't bad. You have touched on a few themes that Pym's biographers, editors, and critics analyse repeatedly: Silly men. Mousy women. Tea. Religion. Quotations. These are worthy of mention. The fact that you still think nothing happens is not. It merely shows that you do not respond to what does happen in the novel, for whatever reason — innocence, feminism, scepticism, youth, cynicism, thoughtlessness, expectation, or too rapid and therefore too shallow reading of the novel — too light, perhaps, a perception of the economy of expression Miss Pym employs.

This is not to say that you must respond to what happens in any particular way nor even like these works; I merely point out that a good many things happen. I will list a few of them:

Three proposals, (plus another, if one counts Bishop Grotes' reconstituted offer to poor Connie Aspinall) two marriages (ditto), self-discovery, self esteem — a little spurt of power. Laughter happens. Some measure of levity happens. Tea is poured, in ritual obeisance to something everyone (at least in this novel) wants, and conveys: a sense of belonging, a place, a value. Tenderness happens – care is given and received. Uncertainties are created – then, miraculously removed. A loved one is remembered. A sense of satisfaction prevails.

Are none of these "events" that you would seek for yourself? If these things happened to *you*, would you regard them all, equally, as nothing?

You ask me again why you should read literature. I feel I should not answer you. It is a question posed by an undergraduate to whom the questioning of established conventions is still a novel and somewhat heady experience undertaken for its own sake. Why ask me? I did not choose your course of study. You could have taken sociology, physics, or architecture. You have circumscribed your own world, for the coming semester at least. There is no point to the question if you yourself cannot answer it. Why *should* you read literature?

Perhaps you should not.

However, I suspect you feel you would like to, and that is the basis of your irritation with silly men, mousy women, tea, religion, and quotations. Is this worthy of the august company of Dante, Proust, Dostoyevsky? It may interest you to know that Barbara Pym felt as you do, when she was about your age – reading Aldous Huxley, and imagining herself in a more glittering, a more significant, world. And so to protect herself from an unbearable exclusion from that world, she wrote a novel, *Young Men in Fancy Dress*, in hope, her biographer says, of becoming part of it.

Her irritation with silly men was no different from yours, or mine, or anyone's really, you see. The only difference is what each of us regards as 'silly.' Literature, or at least, books (I will not presume to add Pym to the Masters, as you call them — although surely there are degrees of literature) offer a way out – out of a time, a space, a life, a status, a level of experience that is unsatisfactory to the reader. Not by virtue of escape, but by metamorphosis, via instruction. As you are being offered a way out of literary exile by the recommended guide — books, maps, and in the end, one hopes, transportation to the inherited literary land of Barbara Pym. And although you may not now want to arrive in such a place, you have chosen it as your destination. But I suppose you must. After all, it does not make sense that you should have chosen to enter a fictional world you find irritating (though you may realise that it is possible to learn something from it).

Oh — but see what Miss Pym's Huxley had to say in *Those Barren Leaves*:' If we wrote it ourselves, we might find Etruscan literature interesting.'

Does it have to be *your* world, Felicity, in order to be habitable, respected, interesting, relevant? 'It's so provincial,' you complained to me of *Some Tame Gazelle* in your first letter. But you see

> ...provincialism does not signify in a writer, and may indeed be the chief source of his strength: only a fool or a prig would complain that Defoe is cockneyfied or Thomas Hardy countrified. But provincialism in a critic is a serious fault. A critic has no right to the narrowness which is the frequent prerogative of the creative artist. He has to have a wide outlook, or he has nothing at all...

I am sorry to keep quoting things at you so seemingly malevolently, but this is what literature does to one after many years — it incorporates, enfolds, enriches one mind with another. Quite a beautiful thing – and very old-fashioned now I'm afraid, except in the most exacting circles among which are such universities as those by which you were privileged to be courted. (That was E. M. Forster, by the way, *Aspects of the Novel*, which, I am sure, someone else will insist that you read. If not, I do.)

As a matter of interest, E.M. Forster went to the same school as my children's father, (which happens to be the school that Jane Austen's father attended) Tonbridge School. In Tonbridge. Not to be confused with Tunbridge

Wells, which was, before Bath was restored, the spa town of the royals and nobles. Tonbridge was also spelled Tunbridge (which you will find mentioned in *Northanger Abbey*, I believe, spelled with a 'u') and there was considerable opposition to its spelling being changed, for such a trivial reason as the avoidance of confusion; interminable postal problems notwithstanding. Tonbridge being a much older town and therefore, to the English, more important (with a Norman castle and sloping keep on the banks of the Medway) such daily irritation was considered a small price to pay for the retention of a 'u.' My dear father-in-law had an office in the castle, you see, and so the 'o/u' controversy is a familiar and familial one. The English of my acquaintance (and Pym's, as you will find) will spend inordinate amounts of energy on an 'o' or a 'u.' Minutiae are their sustenance and, at times, their charm, which is why Pym is so essentially English, whereas Brookner is not.

I recall, for example, a fiery debate that blazed for months in *The Times* correspondence column about whether to put the milk in one's cup before pouring the tea, or after.

By the way, there is a Tonbridge not far from your university, north of Westover. I'm sure there is a connection. As you are in such rich literary country, you will no doubt explore it.

You see, it is really a very large plutocracy, this literature business, wherein fact and fiction are strangely, sweetly at times, interwoven with real life, though you will keep insisting that they are not; a society to which you have applied for membership and to which you bring the current credentials of 'Silly men, mousy women, etc.'

Well done, actually.
So far.

Mallory Cooper

PS: I will predict a response on your part: As an American, you will be stung by the word 'privileged' in this letter (although I did not mean it unkindly – on the contrary, I am delighted when privileges are granted) and you will tell me how hard you worked to be able to get into such an institution. And, perhaps, that everyone 'has a right' to go to college, although you will not tell me why.

You may even invoke the 'follow your dream' philosophy, which has so pervaded the American spirit as to become positively nauseating. And you did work hard(ish). And you probably did deserve to enter a Whitley or a Yarmouth according to the criteria now in vogue for such things. But so did a lot of others who are not there and never will be. Provincialism exists on a national scale, you know. By which I mean that you do not read Greek or Latin; nor have you ever studied classical music, art, or attended any Literature classes beyond the required 'Survey of Literature in English' courses, Shakespeare, Modern Poetry and American Literature classes at an American suburban high school.

Unlike the silly men and mousy women we will address in our next correspondence.

Meanwhile — please begin *Excellent Women*.

December 28, 2_____

My dear Felicity,

What a rapid response! And you have read *Excellent Women*, and *Jane and Prudence*, too. 'More of the same,' you say, albeit with some softening. Yes, that is the joy of reading a particular author, often. One rushes to read the next book, not because it will be entirely different from her previous work, but because it will be similar.

And you are kind to enquire so politely about the origin of my comment on privilege. Yes there is an origin other than pop philosophy. I know a brilliant scholar (Latin, Greek, French, Classics, Mathematics etc. as well as an immeasurable IQ) who applied to Harvard some decades ago. He was not accepted. He was Jewish.

I know it has changed now. Privilege is often simply a matter of birth-date. Let us get back to silliness, mousiness and tea.

I realise, of course, that you are very surprised that I have taken your observations seriously and not begun to lecture you on theme, plot, characters (round and flat), dramatic mode, point of view, language, technique, critical realism, irony, pattern, comic heroism, the nature of feminism in a pre-feminist age, or any other such segment of literary dissection.

This is not because I do not think that these things are important; I do. Within reason. In a limited manner. Well bound by common sense. And in small doses. But you will be made to read the postmodern critics and relevant current critical articles in relevant current academic journals. I need not urge you to do so. But I do urge you to read the works of Ian Watt and E.M. Forster and Virginia Woolf and I.A. Richards and William Empson and F.R. Leavis and Northrop Frye. I strongly suggest that you acquire *The*

Pelican Guide to English Literature (all seven volumes) and books on critical thinking since Plato.

But I must trust that you will be assigned readings from some of these classic literary analysts. At least I hope that is still the case at Yarmouth. I doubt that it has descended into pacifying the ignorant by watering down the curriculum as many universities have. Or descended into the utter nonsense that occupies the fringes of theory. And on that note, you enquired in your last email why I resigned from the last university at which I taught in Britain. Well, quite apart from the pretentious, ridiculous, inane little person who was put in charge (temporarily) of the institution a few months before I left, I simply could not bear the continual lowering of intellectual standards and the truly substandard students that the university accepted in order to ensure a large enough student body to please its financiers.

Of course I had some good students and some excellent ones (and one or two brilliant ones) but I also had a large body of incompetents who should never have been admitted to the academy in the first place. These things and others contributed to my decision to leave what was once a little paradise — only one of a parade of academicians who daily departed from those halls.

I am of course delighted to be Writer in Residence here at Brinley Women's College here in Southern California, with its distinguished faculty, high standards, superior students and, quite frankly, its American common sense, openness, breadth, depth and joy of discovery. I grieve for my colleagues who feel the same way as I did and had no option (in their own minds) but to stay.

But back to literary criticism. I have counted the critical works on my shelves and, for your information and to my surprise, they number three hundred and sixty seven. There are nineteen on Jane Austen alone. And this is in a library of a writer who despises critics. I choose my works carefully, however and include only those written by those who seek to enlighten, not those who set out to prove some minute, befuddled and inconsequential little point, though I do read what I can stomach of the latter. (Library copies. I'd never pay for them.) Literary explication is one thing. Literary stricture is another. However, you will read (and should) legitimate critics as well as biographies of selected authors and cultural histories of their times. You will read both D.H. Lawrence's own work and what he had to say about other writers, Chesterton on the Victorians, and Woolf on everything. You will read, I hope, books like Brownstein's *Becoming A Heroine,* which speaks to women about women and *Literary Friendships in the Age of Wordsworth,* which seems to forget there is a female sex.

But it is not my place to insist that you read these, or that you pass a test or write an essay about them. It is my task to answer your question 'Why read Barbara Pym?' and to help you find your answer to 'Why read Literature at all?' (That is, if, at the end of our correspondence, you still feel in need of an answer).

Therefore we shall begin with your own comments, which, while considering them with due respect, I must point out are guilty of a sweeping generalisation with reference to 'our greatest writers, like Jane Austen, George Eliot…'

You think it is a more worthy pursuit to read Jane Austen and George Eliot than Pym. You may be right. I tend to agree with you, and may therefore be right myself, although it is hardly a matter of alternatives. One may, in perfect conscience, read them all. But it is not because their characters are not silly.

Who in all of Literature is sillier than Mr. Collins? Who more dankly, oppressively, smugly foolish than Mr. Casaubon? The worthiness of being preferred by the literate must lie in something more essential than that. However, to pursue your line of criticism: Silly —
1. Exhibiting a lack of wisdom or good sense; foolish.

2. Lacking seriousness or responsibleness; frivolous.
3. Semiconscious; dazed.

According to the *American Heritage Dictionary*, these are our choices of definition. Let us examine the major male characters in *Some Tame Gazelle* under this trifocal microscope.

Archdeacon Hoccleve: About seventy percent #1 and the rest #2. That is to say, of the percentage of silliness inherent in his character — he is not 100% silly, or Belinda would not care for him. Nor we for Belinda. None of Pym's characters are personifications of any one trait.

Mr. Donne: Mostly #1; Mr. Mold: #1, #2, and by virtue of a permanent state of mild inebriation, a bit of #3; Dr. Parnell: Is he silly? Or simply narrow? Ricardo Bianco: A very small percentage of #3, due to that gentle melancholia which in itself is only a small percentage of his character; Bishop Grote: Largely #1. A bit of #2;

Well, where does that leave us? We agree that the men are silly. They will get sillier. You have read *Jane and Prudence*. Here you have found exaggerated extensions of the Archdeacon in the secular world: the underworked, overtired member of Parliament, Edward Lyall; the lazy and monstrously narcissistic Fabian Driver; as well as another clergyman, Nicholas Cleveland, who, while not silly in the conventional sense, is certainly touched with some fairy dust of dazedness, largely unaware of anything taking place beyond the confines of his skin.

Barbara Pym portrays these men of letters and liturgy with only mild chastisement, but then she did not have to work with them. Such men are easy to tolerate in small social sessions — a lazy afternoon tea here — a brief church meeting there. I have had the misfortune of closer involvement with this degree of ineptitude – and you have had the misfortune of sitting in classes taught by them in your previous institution. Which, is, I understand, why you went to Dr. Hall in the first place, and why you have been sent on to me.

I assure you that you will not meet that dreary myopia at Yarmouth or most other well-regarded colleges or universities, if you choose your courses and teachers wisely.

I must break off here to remind you to tell me which of the novels you are assigned to read, so that we may refer to them. Besides, I have a stack of movies here to review. This leaping between post-war village life in England and eviscerating modern cinema is not the most pleasant of juxtapositions. There is something too schizoid about it. Allow me a few hours with the latest releases, and I shall get back to you.

MC

PS I did pay particular attention to your addendum. I am pleased that you are so moved by Miss Prior in *Some Tame Gazelle*. Indeed, I think that little scene is the most poignant in all of Barbara Pym's novels. And quite the contrary, I do understand that it is difficult to explain exactly why. Perhaps your description 'I felt something foreboding, as soon as I smelled the dead chrysanthemums' is adequate for the time being. We will work on expressing the inexpressible another time.

December 29, 2_____

Dear Felicity,

No, I am not English. What an idea! I am as American as you are. What you detect is flavour, not essence. You asked me why it is that I feel justified in making 'generalisations about the English' when I do not allow you 'the same courtesy' with regard to Barbara Pym. My short answer is that I earned my right to comment (as you have not) by extensive experience, long exposure, deep involvement and voluminous reading. My long answer is this:

I was married for almost twenty years to an English man from Kent (a 'man of Kent' rather than a 'Kentish man' — a distinction that is made by residents according to certain vagaries of the River Medway and on which bank of it one was born). We had four sons.

We lived for much of our time together in English enclaves (within a very segmented and colonial-minded society) in Canada, both in Victoria, British Columbia and Halifax, Nova Scotia. Of those years, we spent several in England.

I studied for many years at British and Canadian universities. The English Department faculty of my undergraduate university was comprised almost entirely of Oxford and Cambridge men (yes, men). They taught me as they had been taught — by Leavis, by Empson - by deeply-educated, highly-talented minds. I also taught in British universities for many years, in England and in Wales. Four of my five degrees are in English Language and Literature, and the only American literature I have ever studied, beyond secondary school, I studied on my own.

We sent our sons (in uniform, with Christopher Robin shoes), to private schools, transported directly (rules, house system, curricula, Latin, rugby, cricket and all) from England to Canada, staffed by English men and women, of which I was on the Boards of Governors whose mandate it was to conserve the traditional way of educating pupils while introducing contemporary subjects to the curricula. My sons' scout troop, 'The Fourth Halifax North British Society Highland Scout Troop' wore kilts, and we all spoke with varying degrees of English accents. After about ten years, particularly when married to an Englishman, it is nearly impossible to avoid a trace. It has largely disappeared now, I believe. The children were corrected if they did not write 'colour' and 'theatre' and pronounce 'Lieutenant' as 'Lef-tenant.'

My in-laws, friends, colleagues, teachers, and neighbours were English. We had the *Manchester Guardian* flown over from England every week; had a subscription to *Punch*; read *The Times* in the University Library most days, and bought our tea at Marks & Spencer when the Fortnum's ran out. I had accounts at Harrods, Fortnum & Mason, Blackwell's Bookshop in Oxford and a number of others I cannot now remember. We ritually observed Sunday Lunch, Boxing Day, Victoria Day, (afternoon) tea.

But I am American. I talk in trains; send things back in restaurants; instigate changes in curriculum, question the crabbed and feeble status quo and have always voted for President by absentee ballot. My first trip after childbirth was not to the baptismal font or to the mohel, but to the American Embassy to register the newborns as 'American Citizens Born Abroad'. I have never curtseyed to royalty, as we have been trained from childhood not to do (Article 1 Section 9 of the Constitution of the United States of America) and would never, ever sing 'God Save the Queen' I respond positively to aggressiveness, innovation, practicality, and improvement to a degree unintelligible to the English, and which, if it were, would be abhorrent to them anyway. Besides, I think they're silly.

Mallory Cooper

December 30, 2_____

Dear Felicity,

Thank you for your letter and your question.

Am I a snob? Yes, probably.

Kind regards,

Mallory Cooper

Dec 31 2_____

Dear Felicity,

In fact, Pym's men can be lumped into several categories, quite easily:

1. The Burdened, an affected, well-educated, semi-leisured upper-middle to lower-upper class (read the Jilly Cooper book) group. These include, broadly, Archdeacon Hoccleve, and a sprinkling of curates (these are the Hoccleves-in-embryo) from *Some Tame Gazelle*; Father Ransome and Sir Denbigh Grote from *A Glass of Blessings*; Aylwin and Neville Forbes, from *No Fond Return of Love*; Basil Branche, who makes a brief but definite appearance in *An Unsuitable Attachment*; and Stephen Latimer from *Crampton Hodnet*. I know now that you are not obliged to read *Crampton Hodnet*, nor *An Academic Question*, nor *Civil to Strangers*, etc., but I expect you will. However, I will stop at Stephen.

2. The Gracious: The gentle, elderly, foreign gentlemen with exquisite manners: Ricardo Bianco from *Some Tame Gazelle*; Luiz MacBride-Pereira from *No Fond Return of Love*; and the Dottore from *An Unsuitable Attachment*.

3. The Earnest: a humourless, occupied, not particularly appealing crowd, often anthropologists; the bitter and obvious product of the single-sex British state school system unredeemed by Oxbridge, experience or money-gauche, irritable, dissatisfied, particularly with women, although they are sometimes even-tempered in a pedestrian sort of way. These include but are not limited to Mervyn Cantrell in *An Unsuitable Attachment*; Mr. Mortlake, Mr. Whiting, and Mr. Oliver in *Jane and Prudence*; Everard Bone in *Excellent Women*; Mr. Coleman in *A Glass of Blessings*;

Mark Penfold and Digby Fox among others, in *Less Than Angels*.

4. The Dull: a neutral, boring, well meaning, dismissible, almost invisible collection: Malcolm Swan, in *Less Than Angels* (clones of whom are alive and well and in the English male population even today); Father Bode, in *A Glass of Blessings*; Mr. Mallet, Teddy Lemon, Mr. Conybeare, in *Excellent Women*.

5. The Husbands: an assortment of non-clergy types, whom one could imagine might be possible for some woman to live with. Rodney Forsyth and Harry Talbot of *A Glass of Blessings*, (already presented to us as husbands), Arnold Root, of the same novel; and Rupert Stonebird and John Challow of *An Unsuitable Attachment*, offered through the eyes of the female protagonists as potential husbands; Geoffrey Manifold of *Jane and Prudence* could be imagined as a husband; and Rocky Napier of *Excellent Women*, whom it is said women desire as a husband. Tom Mallow of *Less than Angels*, had he not died 'in the field' would have been a husband. Though there are others who are husbands, or who marry within or between the novels, they are not worthy or capable of real, sustained, intercommunication with their female counterparts. Jane's Nicholas might be, but he is 'clergy' which, in Pym's world means he is not entirely Jane's husband, but stamped with 'Property of the Church of England'.

6. The Merry, a group of sexually indeterminate fellows, gay perhaps, (it is never specifically stated) and generally cheerful. They are often the most satisfactory company for Pym's women. They see women as people — they notice clothes, hair, food; they are complimentary, companionable, interested, undemanding. They have no particular fears or expectations of women — and therefore come across as

'male girlfriends' in splendid contrast to the uneasy heterosexual antagonists. William Caldicote in *Excellent Women;* James, who seems to have no last name, in *The Sweet Dove Died;* Wilf Bason, Piers Longridge and his friend Keith, in *A Glass of Blessings;* Adam Prince, in *A Few Green Leaves.* While these are widely variant personalities, with a range of educational backgrounds and interests, they do have in common the approbation of women.

7. The Ineffectual, an effete bunch — basically 98% of all Pym men in all novels, but concentrated most strongly in the character of Julian Malory in *Excellent Women.* When one reads the various definitions of effete, a parade of prancing/preening Pym males seem to appear:

1. Depleted of vitality, force, or effectiveness; exhausted.
2. Marked by self-indulgence, triviality, or decadence.
3. Over-refined; effeminate.
4. No longer productive; infertile.

The great exception is Ned in *The Sweet Dove Died* — the only American, the only truly evil character, and the only effective male — who clearly, deliberately sets out to achieve a goal and does. (And I don't think those three characteristics are unrelated in Pym's mind. But that is another matter).

There are, of course, men who fall into several categories, like Humphrey Boyce in *The Sweet Dove Died* — clearly Leonora considers him worthy of her exquisite company; he has been married; seems to disapprove of the notion that James might be gay; and is physically attracted to Leonora, so he may fall into the possible husband category. He is also occupied with a business, which saves him from being entirely inept, but he is curiously ineffectual.

Still, if all the characters could be neatly compartmentalised, this would be *Pilgrim's Progress,* and not a twentieth century novel. (On the other hand, *is* it a twentieth century novel?)

So have we achieved anything? I have made you a list which you can turn into a paper for your seminar ('Perceptions of the Masculine Psyche: The Id in Barbara Pym'?) by finding appropriate quotations from the novels (and they abound) and support from the more acceptable critics, which may be more difficult since few have commented as yet on this topic.

I do not think it would be worth the effort, however, and after all that research, you may find yourself no closer to the answers you seek. I think instead, we must turn to salt. (Not into salt, like Lot's wife, but turn to it, for salvation, as it were.)

And now I really must break off. We are in the midst of viewing foreign films for the Academy Awards, my husband having volunteered for this particular committee, and we should have left for the Academy twenty minutes ago.

To be continued...

Mallory Cooper

December 31, 2_____

Dear Felicity,

Thank you for your letter. I did, in fact, answer your question. It may not have been the answer you expected but it is an answer. Was it an explanation? Of course not. I don't owe you an explanation. Just because you ask a question, it doesn't mean you are entitled to an answer. We have an arrangement – a contract if you like. I am to help you prepare for your seminar and to guide you toward an answer to your two legitimate questions: Why read Barbara Pym and why read literature at all? You are to engage in this interactive process. That's it. I am certainly not obligated to discuss my personal life.

It might help you to know two things, however, and so I will tell them to you:

1. One of the people whose thinking and whose character I respect most in the world was my butcher in remote West Wales.
2. I don't think that everyone or anyone 'deserves' to go to university, but not because it is a privilege that few should be granted. It isn't. Not now. Universities are no longer sacred places, if ever they were. I do think that once, a long time ago, they were sacred to the pursuit of education whereas now, for the most part, they are desultorily engaged in the dispensing of narrow expertise (or, all too often, mere competence) and thus I mourn their demise.

Universities are places where people without skills and talents of other kinds go to be trained for the work that they are able to do. Where once the trivium and quadrivium reigned—and thus the supremacy of interdisciplinary studies; where once these interlacing classics and breathlessly new sciences and burgeoning arts danced and

51

reeled and wed, sit feeble, highly interpretable specialties like some of the 'Film' courses I have experienced. You would not believe what students do not have to know in order to graduate with these degrees. You would not believe what the faculty do not have to know in order to teach them. I am not speaking here of the high-quality well-respected, film programmes offered at USC, UNC, NYU, UCLA and other universities which are staffed by highly-trained, highly-experienced, highly-talented professionals in the film industry. I'm talking about faculty members who have never made a movie, never met anyone who has, and who have never stepped foot in a legitimate movie studio or even been on a lot. They teach their students from the books our friends and colleagues write and have no first hand knowledge of their subject.

Now, I do not meant to suggest that it is a bad thing for people to specialize (even in film) *if they have a special gift*. Aspiring artists go to art schools to perfect inherent talent, dancers and musicians go to Juilliard, for example, to specialize highly, deeply, single-mindedly — and boat-builders are apprenticed to Master boat-builders to hone their own skills and master new ones. The bad thing is that all too often, with regard to universities, inherent skills, talents, ability and potential ability are simply absent. The problem, Felicity, is not that the university is not a respectable institution, though many of them are not. The problem is that it is regarded as such, whereas being a boat-builder, a dancer, a butcher is not. And therein lies hypocrisy.

For there were few academics of my acquaintance in the university adjacent to my butcher's little shop who came near to the standard of excellence in their world that he maintains in his. He knows everything there is to know about his profession, which he learned by apprenticeship (at a very young age) and practice and experience. He works long hours and he gives complete satisfaction to those he serves. He is honest, kind, scrupulous, and certainly forgiving. He has beautiful manners, is perfectly groomed, well aware of what is going on in the wider world, maintains impeccable personal and professional standards, and earns a living in a competitive environment (as opposed to being paid for mediocrity or, worse, tenured despite extraordinary laziness and/or incompetence). And he does not get the summer off. He is bilingual, gentle and often silent. He bears his internal burdens with exceptional fortitude, has both dignity and humility and what is more I have never heard him insult anyone or whine. This is more — much more — than I can say for many of the academics I knew in that place and thus I preferred his company to theirs. And I don't even like meat. Most of my purchases in his shining little shop were eggs and his glossy, perfect, home-grown vegetables.

Many of my closest friends, Felicity, never went to university. Am I a snob? Yes. But not the kind you think.

~M

PS In anticipation of your questions, objections and protestations, let me clarify what I imagine will be the points about which you will have the most questions:

Those who are able should attend university because they are as capable of academic excellence as artists are of original, inventive, art and are as well-endowed with the skills required for excellence in their fields as my butcher is for his. They should go to university because they will thrive there. They should go because they have intellectual fervour, because they are (demonstrably) among the most intellectually acute in the nation, and not because a university degree is a passport to respectability.

My worst students, Felicity, applied to university (to which they should never have been admitted) not because they were academically or creatively gifted, not because they were potential scholars – not because they were intensely interested in Milton or The Victorians or The Romantic Poets or the perfection of the Word. They applied because they were afraid that they would not be as respectable without a university degree as they would be with one – and, they were sadly, largely correct.

How many people do you know who consider a magazine illustrator as respectable as a university professor? A coffee shop owner as intelligent as a doctoral candidate? A furniture maker whose political opinions are as well regarded as a lecturer in medieval tapestries? A butcher whose critical faculties are even recognized , much less well regarded? When there are so many kinds of intelligence – so many talents and skills – and so many people of good character and judgment, it is repugnant that an historical and stupid belief in the supremacy of the university has trained us to give credence to only one.

Let us move on.

December 31, 2_____

Dear Felicity,

Now then — to the topic at hand: In the early days of the Roman Empire, soldiers were paid in salt (sal). This payment was called salarium (salt-money), hence the word 'salary.' Salt could be traded for other goods, of course. It was a currency, as gold is. The value of it was that it preserved food, and therefore life. Salt was absolutely essential to survival. Salt saved lives.

The interesting thing is that the word 'save' comes from the word 'salvation' the root of which is sal — salt. If you took Latin, or even typing, in high school, you will remember the words 'Salve' (pronounced 'salway') or 'salutation.' The former is a greeting; the latter, the name for a greeting. 'Salve' while popularly translated as 'hail' or even 'hello' actually meant 'may you be saved, *preserved* from harm.' Literally, 'may you be salted'.

Which is why we salute, pray for salvation, put salve on our injuries, salvage what we consider worth saving, and why the word 'safe' is a result of this.

When one is safe, it is often because things have been done in a timely manner — the door has been locked before the wolf enters — the fire has been lit after the child moves away from the fireplace. One is often safe because of happiness — which is also aligned to a sort of harmonious timeliness — life may be pleasant, orderly, productive, secure, happy and therefore safe.

It is possible that safety is at times a result of goodness, innocence, simplicity — staying away from addictions or dens of other various iniquities. One is safe because one is simple — does not devise complex or dangerous endeavours or does not stray from the sheltered haven, or the good path. One is often safe, then, because one is timely, innocent, good, simple or (a synonym for simple) silly. Salt (of the earth).

Silly originates from the same root as salt. Salvation. My theory is that you have unwittingly hit upon a most significant aspect of Pym's characters. If nothing else, Pym's men (and women — we have not yet mentioned the quite different silliness of women) are safe. And it is their very silliness that keeps them so. Remember the second definition of silly — 'Lacking in responsibleness.' (Computers, by the way, are interesting. The word 'responsibleness' of which I was instantly suspicious, came out of this very computer's dictionary, and yet when that self-same computer was 'spell-checking' it refused to recognise the word. As well it should have, but there you are — computers are also, on occasion, silly.)

Pym's men are really not responsible. Most of them are financially independent; none of them have children (except Harry Talbot, and he takes Wilmet Forsyth to the pub for a drink — two drinks — while his wife sits in the car with three squirming children on a Saturday morning.) They have no children, but they *are* children, and as such they are fussed over, sought after, cooked for, proposed to, doted on, listened to, praised, indulged, excused, encouraged, and protected like children. They are particularly safe from themselves.

> You have curious things to eat
> I am fed on proper meat
> You must dwell beyond the foam
> But I am safe and live at home

(*I am fed*, you notice, not *I eat.*) Now, this may be a bad thing, or a good thing, or both or neither — but it is an interesting thing. When you first wrote down your reactions to silly men and mousy women, I was tempted to argue that it was not the silliness of men itself, but the conspiracy of

56

silence among intelligent women regarding it that is silly; the conspiratorial, poignant description of which, incidentally, is a major contribution of Pym to the art of the novel. And that thought puts me instantly in mind of Arthur's Education Fund. For it is really that which typifies the cycle of salt to silliness, from safety to safety.

Arthur's Education Fund is Virginia Woolf's euphemism for the oppression of women over the centuries, representing in its generic title the habit of salting away every ounce of energy and money for a boy's future without the merest scrap of concern about that of his sister. Arthur, at least will be taken care of. Arthur, it seems, will be safe.

He will end up being a soldier and the army will take care of him; or a clergyman, and the church will oblige; or a professor, wherein the university will claim him, and he will spend a good many hours of his life in the company of his fellows, unaware of or unconcerned about the responsibilities, activities and burdens of his spouse if he has one. He may not have to become anything other than older, in which case it is highly likely that some estate or land has been entailed to him, and will keep him occupied in an even smaller environment.

And he will almost certainly be married to someone else's deprived sister, so that the cycle is perpetuated. She will already have been trained by her brothers to expect nothing. Arthur will have been saved from the responsibility for her needs. She will have none.

There is, in *Three Guineas* (which I urgently recommend) a passage that might have been written by any of Pym's heroines, although it belongs, in expression at least, to Virginia Woolf. It is long and we are fast approaching another year, but it is worth some of the few remaining moments of this dying year to read this again:

> How many, how splendid, how extremely
> ornate they are—the clothes worn by the

educated man in his public capacity! Now you dress in violet; a jewelled crucifix swings on your breast; now your shoulders are covered with lace; now furred with ermine; now slung with many linked chains set with precious stones.

Now you wear wigs on your heads; rows of graduated curls descend to your necks. Now your hats are boat shaped, or cocked; now they mount in cones of black fur; now they are made of brass and scuttle shaped; now plumes of red, now of blue hair surmount them. Sometimes gowns cover your legs; sometimes gaiters.

Tabards embroidered with lions and unicorns swing from your shoulders; metal objects cut in star shapes or in circles glitter and twinkle upon your breasts. Ribbons of all colours—blue, purple, crimson—cross from shoulder to shoulder... every button, rosette and stripe seems to have some symbolic meaning. Some have the right to wear plain buttons only; others, rosettes; some may wear a single stripe; others three, four, five or six.

And each curl or stripe is sewn on at precisely the right distance apart; it may be one inch for one man, one inch and a quarter for another. Rules again regulate the gold wire on the shoulders, the braid on the trousers, the cockades on the hats—but no single pair of eyes can observe all these distinctions, let alone account for them accurately...

...A woman who advertised her motherhood by a tuft of horsehair on the left shoulder would scarcely, you will agree, be a venerable object. (Pg. 24-25 — The Penguin edition.)

These are some of the men that Barbara Pym knew, and I know, and whom, if you do not know them now, you will almost certainly meet. They are not yet extinct, Brad Pitt notwithstanding. (I am off in another minute to screen the latest releases, and see in the New Year.) And if you think that the above quotation refers to a small percentage of the English population, you are right. But the attitude does not — some cultural habits extend beyond class or economic lines. All over England, even in the poorest of families, the law of precedence has been historically and to a surprising extent has remained until very recently, 'males first,'

There was no girl over the age of twelve or thirteen living permanently at home. Some were sent out to their first place at eleven. The way they were pushed into the world at that tender age might have seemed heartless to a casual observer.

As soon as a little girl approached school leaving age, her mother would say, 'About time you was earnin' your own livin', me gal' or to a neighbour, 'I shan't be sorry when our young so and so gets her knees under somebody else's table. Five slices for breakfast this mornin', if you please!'

From that time onward, the child was made to feel herself one too many in the overcrowded home, while her brothers, when they left school, were treated with new respect and made much of. (Flora Thompson. *Lark Rise to Candleford*, Penguin edition, pg. 155.)

Hence we will proceed, Felicity, on the first day of the New Year, to mousy women.

Mallory Cooper

January 1, 2_____, (9:00 am)

Dear Felicity,

You may be right. I think attending the Rose Bowl takes precedence. We will resume tomorrow. Have fun.

—*M. Cooper*

Mousy Women

January 2, 2_____

Dear Felicity,

Yes, I did read your remarks about my remarks about Virginia Woolf's remarks about men. I do not recall having said that I agree with Ms. Woolf. Or that I do not. Nor am I interested in discussing feminism except insofar as it relates to Barbara Pym. And so, while I thank you for the compliment, I must ask you to keep to the work at hand. The new semester begins in three weeks. That should alarm you.

And do respond next time with something sensible about your own reading of the novel. You will not learn much if your only participation in this process is reactive.

As to your question, 'How do I choose my professors wisely?' You must read what they write, of course. You wouldn't trust the tutelage of a Professor of Neurosurgery who had never practised surgery, or a piano teacher who did not know how to play the piano or a driving instructor who had never driven a car. Why would you care to be taught Literature by people who have never produced any? (fiction or non.) You will hear the argument that they are there to teach you how to deconstruct a novel or a poem, and that they are able to do that without ever having written anything themselves. Well, if you want to buy that, you are free to do so.

And there are times and places when and where it is not entirely untrue. Some are better readers than writers and can convey that ability to students. It was more likely to be true in the past, when one's professors could be relied upon to hold the entire history of English Literature in their heads. But it is rare, very rare, to be able to truly understand something that one has never done. Just remember that any idiot can take a hatchet to the Pieta or a book. Few who do so can create one. Also, you might want to find out if your professors can relate their own area of expertise to another — another era or form of Literature — another voice in the poetic lineage — another discipline entirely. If they cannot, they are not educated and you must not trust them with the solemn task of educating you. They may be brilliant little myopics, but they are myopics all the same. I trust that is not your aim.

Mallory Cooper

January 3, 2_____

Dear Felicity,

Your observations, entitled 'Excellent (Mousy) Women' have some merit. I would like you to keep this in mind, lest you feel unnecessarily discouraged by my next comment, which is that I am not going to read them. Oh, I began to read and evaluate them—and then I realised that I was putting far more effort into your work than you had, so I stopped. However, you are welcome to my commentary on your first four paragraphs, and my conclusion, which is that if this is what you think an essay is, you may prefer another discipline.

Mallory Cooper

Excellent (Mousy) Women
by Felicity Halper

Clothes play an important role in Excellent Women. They reinforce the state of mind we find these characters in, and grant us insight into their narrow lives as single women '...I, mousy and rather plain anyway, drew attention to these qualities with my rather shapeless overall and old fawn skirt.' (EW pg. 7)

Mildred Lathbury begins to be interested in her appearance after she meets the Napiers, one of whom is a handsome husband-figure she unconsciously wishes were hers. 'I suppose I had taken to using a little more make-up, my hair was more carefully arranged, my clothes a little less drab.' (pg. 100)

Her closest friend, Dora, however, has no such reason to change her character. She undergoes no such metamorphosis and remains content in the role of spinster school-teacher:

> *'Dora decided to do some washing before supper and within half an hour the kitchen was festooned with lines of depressing looking underwear—fawn lock-knit knickers and petticoats of the same material. It was even drearier than mine.' (pg. 105-106)*

Pym's women are dependent on the men around them to elevate their appearance, as we have seen in Some Tame Gazelle where Belinda and Harriet Bede dress up only for the Archdeacon and his curates.

Let us look at each of your four statements:
1. 'Clothes play an important role in *Excellent Women*. They reinforce the state of mind we find these characters in, and grant us insight into their circumscribed lives as single women.'

You have an interesting idea here — it is quite possible that the clothes 'these women' choose (if they had a choice, and that was sometimes not the case in post war England) reinforce 'their state of mind'. But you have not said what that state is. Neither have you made it clear who these women are, nor if there is, indeed, one state of mind in which they are all either mired or joyfully ensconced — your reader has no idea whether their (or her) mental/emotional condition is a welcome one. You indicate that this state is brought on by these grim garments.

On the other hand, assuming that there are several women in the novel who are in the same drab condition, it is equally possible that 'their state of mind' is the *raison d'être* for the clothes and not the reverse. The use of 'reinforce' with its architectural suggestion of strength and buttresses is not perhaps as clear as it could be here — conceivably a gentler word is needed to indicate cause and effect, or at least confluence between the inner and outer woman.

However, this is rather a quibble on my part, since you do end up with an appropriate quotation, which does 'reinforce' the point I believe you are trying to make; that Mildred (whom you did not identify) is physically plain, a fact that is magnified by her sartorial dowdiness. So the quotation you employ ('...I, mousy and rather plain anyway, drew attention to these qualities with my rather shapeless overall and old fawn skirt.') is a good choice.

'We find these characters in' should be changed to 'in which we find these characters.' Also 'clothes' do not 'grant' us insight or anything else, in this sentence. They have no power of bequest. They may be symbols or indicators, but it is Pym who performs the action here. Really, Felicity — I cannot believe you don't know this — you must have been tired — or in some other enfeebled condition when you wrote this.

Now let us examine what one of Barbara Pym's contemporaries had to say about dowdiness. I happened to come across some old copies of *Punch* in the UCLA Library the other day, while I was doing some research on Anita Brookner. Fortunately there were several from the fifties, so

66

I chose one at random from 1958, the year in which Barbara Pym was writing *No Fond Return of Love*. Here is an excerpt of an article entitled 'Speech Days', written by Alison Adburgham:

Referring to the Fourth of June at Eton, a newspaper correspondent mentioned 'the distinguished dowdiness' of some of the parents. We know exactly what he meant, but are inclined to argue that an essential quality of dowdiness is the absence of distinction. A duchess may look like a scarecrow, but she has good bones; and, as with the scarecrow, the bones show through.

> Dowdiness has no bones. It is a flabby condition brought on by temperament, environment, and other contributory factors. For instance, a disregarded or broken heart in youth may be responsible for the disregarding of broken shoulder-straps in middle-age; the early wrecking of ambitions responsible for the later wrinkling of stockings. (*The Pick of Punch*, 1958. Pg. 48-49)

Here would be an excellent opportunity for you to expand your idea of cause and effect — the 'clothes maketh the man' theory. Of course you did not come across this article, but it might have occurred to you to look for something to substantiate your views. I do hope you have not fallen into the insupportable habit of thinking that your own analysis of any work of literature is sufficient for academic purposes. You may concur with or depart from the opinions of established writers, reviewers, (some) literary critics, but you may not ignore them. In any case, in order to dispute an opinion, one must have become cognisant of it.

And do not come back to me with the complaint that I asked you for a sensible response based on your own reading of the novel. 'Based on' does not mean 'entirely comprised of' and what you have written is not sensible.

2. Your next statement: 'Mildred Lathbury begins to be interested in her appearance after she meets the Napiers, one of whom is a handsome husband-figure she unconsciously wishes were hers' is debatable. While it is true that Mildred's wish to be less drab is manifested after she meets the Napiers, it is not true that her desires are unconscious. Consider this passage:

> I suppose it must have been the Nuits St. Georges or the spring day or the intimate atmosphere of the restaurant, but I heard myself to my horror, murmuring something about Rocky Napier being just the kind of person I should have liked for myself. (EW, pg. 69)

Or, the even more emphatically:

> After he had gone I stood looking out of the window until his taxi was out of sight.
>   The effects of shock and grief are too well known to need description and I stood at the window for a long time. At last I did make a cup of tea but I could not eat anything... (EW, pg. 167)

'Shock' and 'grief' are powerful indications of Mildred's awareness of her feelings for Rocky Napier, who, incidentally, is not a 'handsome husband-figure'. (By the way, what made you use such awkward phrasing. It doesn't even sound like you — at least not in the letters I receive from you.) Rocky is a husband, not a husband-figure, whatever that is, and yes, he is very handsome, quite apart from his marital status. A handsome 'husband-figure' could be interpreted to mean that the character of Rocky Napier is an archetypal symbol of a husband and, as such, is handsomely portrayed by Barbara Pym. A 'handsome-husband' figure is perhaps what you meant. But it would still have been out of place. As is the quantifying relative pronoun phrase, 'one of whom' (is a handsome husband-figure) which allows for the possibility that the 'other of whom' is an ugly husband-figure.

Your support from the text is good — 'I suppose I had taken to using a little more make-up, my hair was more carefully arranged, my clothes a little less drab.' (pg. 100) Mildred does, in fact, take more trouble to appear less dowdy after meeting the Napiers, although I think you will find that Helena Napier was in some measure responsible for Mildred's self-improvement programme. Helena is a kind of sartorial gauge, as it were, since before her arrival, Mildred's clothes and make-up compared favourably with the scatty Winifred, 'dressed, as usual in an odd assortment of clothes, most of which had belonged to other people' (EW pg. 13) and the stolid, unappealing, Dora.

3. Your third paragraph is 'Her closest friend Dora, however, has no such reason to change her character. She undergoes no such metamorphosis and remains content in the role of spinster school-teacher.' Well. Here is an interesting point. Does one's character change by changing one's clothes? I would tend to think not. One's demeanour may be affected, (as many actresses have mentioned when playing period roles, crammed into corsets and bustles); or one's behaviour modified by the unexpected freedom or restraint of particular garments but not one's character. I believe not only that Mildred's character remained constant, but that that very constancy is the point of the novel. Therefore your selection, while apt enough in describing Dora, is apropos of nothing, including, by the way, her

spinsterhood, in which state you may find any number of chic women, or her profession, which does not automatically condemn her to the appalling garments described here:

> 'Dora decided to do some washing before supper and within half an hour the kitchen was festooned with lines of depressing looking underwear – fawn lock-knit knickers and petticoats of the same material. It was even drearier than mine'. (pg. 105-106)

But keep that page marked. You may need it for a real essay.

4. Now to the last paragraph: 'Pym's women are dependent on the men around them to elevate their appearance, as we have seen in *Some Tame Gazelle* where Belinda and Harriet Bede dress up only for the Archdeacon and his curates.'

There is no point in bringing up *Some Tame Gazelle* at this point. We haven't been properly introduced to the cast of *Excellent Women* yet. Besides, Belinda and Harriet do not dress up as a duo — in a unified performance — for this collection of men.

Harriet chooses her dress with care only for the one reigning curate in her life (they are singular and serial). She despises the Archdeacon, remember. And Belinda, in her shapeless and faded blue chiffon, (because, 'Henry had once said that he liked her in pale colours, and although that had been over thirty years ago, it was possible that he still might...' STG pg. 115) adorns herself only for the Archdeacon.

Besides, you are stating a conclusion for which you have as yet given no basis, and I, for one, not having been sufficiently aroused to curiosity by your opening remarks, am disinclined to pursue the subject. Furthermore, I have reason to believe from your letters that your interest in

Barbara Pym's work lies elsewhere. You need not write about aspects of her work that do not interest you. There is plenty of material concerning the role of the church in her novels, to occupy your mind.

I think you may be disturbed or discouraged by these remarks. If the former, good. If the latter, no need. We all have 'off' days. I am assuming that this is the result of one of yours. Try again.

MC

January 4, 2_____

Dear Felicity,

I don't think I am particularly harsh. On the contrary, I feel a great and benevolent responsibility toward you. I want you to do well. And you don't need me to bolster your self-esteem — this is nonsense. All you have to do to get the 'emotional support' you say (but do not mean) that you want, is to rush to your iphone and tweet away. In an instant you will get a sufficient number of indignant and ignorant little digitisms from your friends in response to my insensitivity, in order to restore your self-regard. I am not interested in how you feel about my remarks. I am interested in how you think. And write. You will get praise when you deserve it.

It was a poor essay and all the kind remarks and telling you 'all the things you did right' (not much) is not going to change that. Rewarding poor performance encourages it — a fact reinforced early in my undergraduate life, the day our marked essays (for 17th Century Poetry and Prose) were due. My iconic and revered professor (himself a former student of FR Leavis at Cambridge) walked into the classroom with a great sheaf of essays from which he meticulously extracted three that he placed ominously on the desk. He said, 'I evaluated your essays and have given each of them what they deserve.' He then dumped the entire pile of essays into the wastepaper basket and left the room. No one moved. Several minutes passed in silence and when he did not come back, the entire class (about 36 of us) almost tiptoeing (for what reason it is hard to say) and still in complete silence, went to the wastepaper basket to retrieve what Professor Terry would certainly *not* have called essays. I am pleased now, though I was too numb to be pleased at the time, to say that mine was not among them. It was one of the three on the desk. But I got the message as clearly and as chillingly as everyone else.

Do the essay again.

Now, Hilary Pym, Barbara's sister, writes in *A Very Private Eye — An Autobiography in Diaries and Letters,* that clothes were 'an abiding passion' of Barbara. That being the case, one may wonder why most of her heroines disdain fashion as being somehow an unworthy pursuit. The answer is, of course, an intricate one.

Let us begin first with our Puritan heritage. There has been historically a strong spiritual and cultural strain of belief in England, as in the fledgling United States, that a too avid interest in the outer trappings ('too avid' being a relative term and in this case denoting even the mildest of attentions) may deflect focus from the inner man. Or woman. It proceeds from the necessary avoidance of one of the Seven Deadly Sins: Pride. (The others being, as your church will have no doubt informed you, Sloth, Gluttony, Envy, Avarice, Wrath and Lust.) As most of Pym's female protagonists are relatively well-educated churchgoers, they would have been warned against this and other vices from the pulpit and in their penchant for classical works.

> Perhaps I was getting spinsterish and 'set' in my ways, but I was irritated at having been woken. I stretched out my hand toward the little bookshelf where I kept cookery and devotional books, the most comforting bedtime reading. My hand might have chosen *Religio Medici*, but I was rather glad that it had picked out *Chinese Cookery*, and I was soon soothed into drowsiness. (EW, pg. 20)

Since *Religio Medici* is beside Mildred Lathbury's bed, and is considered to be among 'the most comforting bedtime reading,' we can assume her intimate acquaintance with it.

Therefore, it behoves us to become somewhat familiar with it if we are to examine the characteristics of Pym's 'mousy women' (your term, remember!) Its author, Sir Thomas Browne (b. Oct. 19, 1605, d. Oct. 19, 1682) was an Anglican physician, concerned with reconciling science and religion.

Religio Medici (1643) is a particularly poetic, and illuminating prose work — a charming self-revelation, written basically to expose some of the commonly held myths of the day: for example, 'that salamanders live in fire, that ostriches digest iron and that Aristotle drowned himself in the Euripus because he could not explain its tides' according to the synopsis given at your favourite internet resource, Wikipedia, which, I am sure I need not remind you, is neither a sufficient nor respectable academic reference. However, it *is* an excellent source from which to gather statements that you can subsequently verify via legitimate academic resources. Back to *Religio Medici*, one splendid effect of its clear process of reason and logic, fundamental to Browne's system of personal observation, is the extent to which subsequent writers were the beneficiaries of its literary style, a style that you would do well to examine. In any case, he had some odd fixations — one of which was the joy of insignificance.

'To be nameless in worthy deeds exceeds an infamous history,' he wrote (in *Hydriotaphia*, 1658). 'The Caananitish woman lives more happily without a name than Herodias with one.'

We can well imagine Mildred pondering the virtues of obscurity in the late evening hours in her solitary bed, as it seems to be a state to which she feels by turns relegated and called:

> ...unmarried women with no ties could very well become unwanted... for who was there to grieve for me when I was gone? Dora, the Malorys, one or two people in my old village

might be sorry, but I was not really first in anybody's life... (EW pg. 39)

We cannot assume that one's interest in *Religio Medici* is directly proportional to one's mousiness, however; although Margaret Drabble does have a point, in *A Summer Birdcage*, in which the following dialogue occurs between two very beautiful Oxford-educated sisters:

> 'I've always fancied you as a don' said Louise. 'I used to fancy myself as one. But I'll tell you what's wrong with that. It's sex. You can't be a sexy don. It's all right for men, being learned and attractive, but for women, it's a mistake. It detracts from the essential seriousness of the business... you'd soon find yourself playing it down instead of up if you wanted to get to the top, and when you've got only one life that seems a pity.' (pg. 183-4 Penguin ed.)

Still, these un-mousy characters also quote the classics throughout their novels as do Pym's mousy ones, and most certainly would be acquainted with *Religio Medici*—the point being, of course, that mousiness can be nothing more than a deliberate attitude. The speaker above espouses the same doctrine, indeed comes from the same world, as Barbara Pym (albeit some years later). She simply makes a different choice.

Second, in early post-modern England (the Carnaby Street era notwithstanding) a certain intellectual disdain for anything that smacked of glamour had woven its way into even the secular culture. At middle to upper-class English girls' schools, (the product of which we are examining in Pym's novels) it was not the most feminine, nor the most sartorially attractive (within a very small range of options, since these schools require uniforms) girl who won the approbation of her mistresses or peers. It was the one who, like her brothers, endured field hockey injuries without whimpering, or when wrongfully blamed for some school infraction, refrained manfully (intentional use of the word) from 'ratting.'

While these cultural attitudes may have been modified in those institutions in the years since I was last resident in England, they were certainly in full flower during the decades in which the novels are set.

Those of weaker moral or physical stamina are very often portrayed in children's literature as being preoccupied with looks, finery, and baubles; and consequently are unpleasantly vain. Search through the still popular Enid Blyton's 'school series' *First Term at Malory Towers, Upper Fourth at St. Clare's*, etc. for stereotypical heroines versus the school airheads (who by the way are often American or French girls, transferred in for a term or two). You will find no better source. Generations of girls — even those of less affluence or social status — have grown up on these novels and hence on this underlying disposition. I am not saying these are worthy reading. Simply that millions read them.

Noel Streatfield's novels for children, widely sold in the United States where they fail to be supported by the culture and so end up as a charming glimpse into a different way of life, are also fine examples of the limits that segment of English society imposed on personal vanity. A wish to be reasonably attractive and appropriately dressed is one thing (though it was deemed morally superior not to wish it at all) but to aspire to outright beauty and head-turning allure is another. Again, it is often the American import in these books whose vanity is rampant, whose vacuity is frankly unbelievable and whose self-regard is grossly over-inflated. Hence the heritage of a surprisingly distorted view of Americans that many of my students, colleagues and even friends in the UK seemed to have. On the other hand, it helps to actually *know* some Americans if not to be in

America for a reasonable amount of time (not five days in Disneyworld) before making pronouncements on 300 million people. The entire United Kingdom could fit into California and leave enough square miles left over for Denmark and The Republic of Macedonia (or most of Switzerland). I found it peculiar that, as the USA is two and a half times the size of the entire European Union and much more geographically diverse, those with (again) little or no experience of it, would rely on these flimsy depictions as cultural guides. I doubt if anyone would judge all of Europe on Babar or Paddington Bear.

A third reason for this curious tendency toward what results in later life in 'mousiness,' is that it was considered somewhat unpatriotic (both during the height of the British Empire and after the Second World War) to display leanings toward anything which Britain could not (or did not) produce. Stunning clothes; enticing cosmetics; a Hollywood sheen on the hair, teeth, eyes, and figures of the women of England were not valued. Since England appropriated to itself large portions of the world with all their glittering resources — diamonds in Africa, silks in China, etc., it seems somewhat odd if not supremely hypocritical to generally eschew them, but there it is. The English are nothing if not odd.

Jilly *Cooper*, in her acerbic book, *Class*, observes that:

> Traditionally, the aristocracy survived because they were the wiliest of the tribe and knew when to lie low. Let the nouveau riche swagger around in their finery, showing off their wealth and getting their heads chopped off by royalty, or later by revolutionaries.

> Harry Stow-Crat's [Cooper's euphemism for the upper class male] ancestors were prepared to dress up when the King commanded it;

77

otherwise they camouflaged themselves and blended in with their surroundings. Today Harry is only copying his forebears when he wears a dark suit in the grey of London, and green, dung-coloured or brown clothes in the country...

...Traditionally, too, because the upper classes believe in supporting their own industries, they regard anything that's lived — wool, leather, silk, cotton as all right, but anything man-made — crimplene, polyester or plastic—as decidedly vulgar... (Class, pg.274)

Another aspect of mousiness can trace its origins to war. If, as the Duke of Wellington declared, the Battle of Waterloo was won on the playing fields of Eton, so too the Battles of World War II in England were won by the immense collective courage, sacrifice, and unity on the home front, which all British women experienced.

Years of living and working together under the shadows of air raids, bombs, and deprivation of even basic necessities, left their legacy on subsequent decades. Notwithstanding the fact that the 'playing fields of Eton' philosophy was just as stringently applied at girls' schools throughout the country, it was also the lifeblood of a nation under attack. With that kind of dire unity, a particularly tenacious bond forms.

There was no room for prima donnas in the bomb shelters and bread lines of England. And no reason for one woman to try to seriously outshine another — not to mention the fact that there was very little money available to buy stylish clothes and cosmetics, even if they had been accessible. Therefore, a general consensus that shabbiness was one of the costs of victory, and not a particularly high price to pay, created a spirit among British women that to some extent exists today, at least among those who were there or subsequently felt its consequences. Certainly an unflagging team spirit lay loyally beneath the social surface during Barbara Pym's post-war lifetime. The British lost 92,673 civilians in the war. Mothers putting children to bed, schoolchildren doing prep (homework) — you know the rest. And if you don't, you should.

For whatever characteristics are called to mind when the English of Barbara Pym's era are mentioned, the first one should be spectacular, heroic — and poignant — courage. Perhaps, with such internal accoutrements, external ones are less important.

Our highly individualistic and fiercely competitive media-centric American culture (and the fact that we have never had to huddle together under plane-dark skies) is not, and never has been, particularly receptive to collective mousiness. But a sense of collectiveness is what all Pym's real heroines have, and to depart too radically from that norm, is to be somehow not quite orthodox, even disloyal.

Don't forget that the effects of war in England — and Scotland and Wales and Northern Ireland, persisted throughout the early fifties. My own contemporaries, who were born well after VE Day, easily recall rationing, playing games among bombsites, the restraint of constant economy, and a general socio-political atmosphere of careful frugality. And, since five of the eight novels published during Barbara Pym's lifetime were written in the fifties, you will find this same ambience in them.

Of course there are beautiful, elegant, tasteful women in Pym's novels — but there are no stunning, glamorous, sexy women. When the former do appear, they usually lose. Allegra Gray in *Excellent Women* is such a woman:

> Mrs. Gray was, as I had supposed from my first
> glimpse of her, good-looking and nicely

dressed, rather too nicely dressed for a clergyman's widow... (EW, pg. 57)

Or consider the moral dilemma of Wilmet in *A Glass of Blessings*, one sunny spring afternoon:

> I was wearing a dress of deep coral-coloured poplin, very simple, with a pair of coral and silver earrings, and a bracelet to match. I always like myself in deep clear colours and I felt at my best now and wondered if people were looking at me as I passed them. They seemed to be lovers mostly absorbed in each other. I did not mind this but when a drab-looking woman in a tweed skirt and crumpled pink blouse looked up from her sandwich and *New Statesman*, I felt suddenly embarrassed... What could her life have held? (GB, Pg. 189)

There is even an entire Pym novel devoted to the downfall of elegance, beauty and taste, personified in the character of the colossally self-preoccupied Leonora whose interest in so simple an activity as attending a flower show, lay in

> ...the sight of such large and faultless blooms, so exquisite in colour, so absolutely correct in all their finer points...a comfort and satisfaction to one who loved perfection as much as she did. Yet, when one came to think of it, the only flowers that were really perfect were those, like the peonies which went so well with one's charming room, that had the added grace of having been presented to oneself. (SDD pg. 208)

So — we have the beginnings of a background (which you will have to augment for your studies) for the preponderance of mousy women in Barbara Pym's novels and, should you wish to explore it, in English novels in general. You have no doubt read *Jane Eyre* and may detect the faintest hint of its heritage in Barbara Pym's work. Miss Pym, however, will have her own reasons for allowing the mouse centre stage. As we shall see.

Mallory Cooper

PS I do not mean to suggest that these themes of Vanity vs. Virtue or The Haves vs. The Have-nots began with World War II. Aesop wrote the Tortoise and the Hare in the 6th century BC, and 2500 years later, Anita Brookner is still writing it. But I do think that we cannot ignore the immediate effects of deprivation and loss in these quiet stories. Barbara Pym observed what was before her, and however frivolously she appeared to regard the war, (in her autobiographical material, all she seems to do during her stint as a WREN in the war is eat, flirt and dance) she could not fail to notice its repercussions on others.

January 5, 2_____

Dear Felicity,

You quite mistake me. I am not 'casting aspersions' on a 'healthy interest in one's appearance.' And I have no way of knowing what your clothes look like. I have never met you. I merely point out that in Barbara Pym's world, dowdiness is not entirely unconnected to virtue. I am personally well-disposed towards good looks, and certainly do not 'discount them.' How could I? I work in Hollywood, remember!

Moving from Berkeley to Los Angeles — from limp hair and hemp to plastic surgery and universal gloss — I have seen both ends of a (not wildly important) spectrum. I'm not sure which is more repellent — the self-righteous rigor with which the former pursue plainness; or the colossal, almost religious, self-preoccupation of the latter.

I happen to think that one should look as good as one can, but not go into hysterics about it. And of course I am not suggesting that you aspire to be dowdy so that other people will think you intelligent. They will know that anyway as soon as you open your mouth. It is true you will have a harder time than most. You are a very pretty girl, from the photograph I have seen in your file. I know what you are up against. I have had my share of prejudice in academia, being more than reasonably good looking in my younger days. A poorly-disguised bitchiness from one or two female departmental colleagues was certainly in play even in my recent experience — all those little pinpricks and exclusions that the small-minded fondly imagine will punish, exhort or inspire one into being plainer. Beauty, to many English academics, is an affront and a certain indication that brains have been sacrificed to it. (It's all that Enid Blyton again.) Things are usually a little different between the sexes, though that hardly helps the situation. But then, jealousies abound everywhere. You will need to know where your best

82

interests lie, and dress/camouflage to that end, if you wish to play academic or any other games.

All I am suggesting is that Pym's heroines represent their interests accurately by not appearing at their Women's Institute meetings in shiny violet, skin-tight polyester mini-skirts, grunge make-up and nose-rings. But you illustrate my point. You are not a middle-aged English spinster living a village or circumscribed city life in the 1950s. It is therefore possible that you may well represent your interests, such as they are, by such outstanding raiment.

You are 19 years old.

This is America.

Wear what you wish.

However, whatever your attire, your assignment is to investigate the leitmotif (and there may be more than one) of each novel and indeed to investigate every reference to every author, book, poem or source quoted in Barbara Pym's work. You will not understand her characters, nor will you succeed in your English Literature studies unless you do. Speaking of which, please look up the origins of 'casting aspersions.'

Thank you for your good wishes for the New Year. I accept and return them.

Mallory Cooper

January 7, 2_____

Dear Felicity,

You have done well with your lists and your questions. This is the kind of response that demonstrates serious involvement with the novels, as well as the fact that you have now read *No Fond Return of Love, Less than Angels* and *A Glass of Blessings*. So now, as you point out, we have many references to clothes and mousiness in these and other novels and an 'ambiguous attitude toward them.' Yes. Quite.

The ambiguity is absolutely necessary — not simply as a reflection of the varying responses to outward appearance, which play such a large part in all of the novels, but also as a literary device. There is no texture without ambiguity, no perspective without the distance it lends. William Empson in his now classic *Seven Types of Ambiguity* outlines the significance of ambiguity:

> We call it ambiguous... when we recognise that there could be a puzzle as to what the author meant, in that alternative views might be taken without sheer misreading... any verbal nuance, however slight, which gives room for alternative reactions to the same piece of language. (pg 70)

Each of the seven types is explored in its own chapter, with which you will become familiar, as I intend to suggest at a later date that you examine them.

Take the ambiguity of mousiness, for example. The word is not precisely complimentary. Nor is it precisely uncomplimentary. In fact, there are occasions when it can be, and is, used as an endearment, as in the case of Blanche Vernon's husband Bertie, who defected from their twenty year marriage to the adorable, sexy, pert, and ultimately intolerable charms of his girl-friend, Mousie, in Anita Brookner's *Misalliance*. There, certainly, the word is ambiguous. And, being Brookner, very deliberate.

I doubt if Mrs. Tittlemouse would find the word 'mousy' objectionable, and perhaps the thousands of children (of all classes, races and nationalities) who have been delighted by Beatrix Potter's *The Tale of Mrs. Tittlemouse* would concur with that view.

'Why,' you ask (underlined) with regard to *Some Tame Gazelle*, 'Would anyone make such an effort to remain so colourless and obscure?'

Hmm. Here comes the word Americans hate and yet practise every day: Class. Part of the answer to your question has to do with social stratum (strata, actually). Let us look at colour first.

You now have the Jilly Cooper book, *Class*. Turn to page 274: '...on the whole, the aristocracy's hair is a sort of light brown, upper class mouse.' Not quite a derogatory statement. It exists in reference to its sister sentences under the same heading of 'Appearance,' and follows (and is therefore flavoured by) this thought:

> If there is one single class indicator it is colour. The upper classes tend not to wear crude, garish, clashing colours. Not for them the dayglo oranges or reds, the jarring lime greens and citrus yellows, the royal blues, mauves and cyclamen pinks...

Or, as Miss Pym delicately puts it: 'It was noticeable that...the older members of the *villagers'* [my italics] party were wearing newer, smarter clothes than the rector and his group.'(FGL pg. 6)

And don't be misled by the word 'smarter.' The English can make any word derogatory, but have a particular talent for inversion — that is, using an unmistakably positive word offensively.

'How *absorbing* for you.'

'May I congratulate you, Minister, on a most *courageous* decision.'

'*What* a remarkable hat.'

'Mary has joined the Girl Guides. *Most* energetic.'

'It *does* suit you.'

'*Such* a clever boy.'

Et cetera. (The italics indicate the emphasis in the spoken sentence, not necessarily the positive/negative word.) Occasionally very funny. Often cruel. Invariably linked to a needle-sharp awareness, on the part of the user, of the nuance, rather than the definition of an English word. And of course indicative of the narrow experience and/or mind of the speaker.

A case in point is Leonora's observation of class-implied-by-colour, when she encounters the following:

> ...a man and two small boys accompanied by Mum and perhaps Gran in white orlon cardigans, with the bright floral prints of their dresses showing through them. How did such people manage to get off in the week? Leonora wondered. (SDD pg. 37)

Here Leonora's snide internal commentary is indicated not only by Barbara Pym's use of the words 'bright floral prints' or even 'white orlon' (which was, in that era, an implausible electric-white synthetic material) but also by her use of 'Mum' and 'Gran' — affectionate names when used by (what Pym's characters tend to think of as) the lower classes and inverted, unpleasant labels when used by the upper.

Phoebe's cushions, in the same novel are considered 'bright and garish — not at all the sort of thing anyone one knew would choose.'(pg. 63)

There are (perhaps unintentional) comic passages depicting class within the novels. When Nicholas Cleveland looks out of his study window and remarks that 'there is a lady, no perhaps a woman, in a straw hat with a bird on it...' coming up the walk, (JP, pg. 17) it would appear that a lady and a woman belong to different genders. But Nicholas is merely being precise in his language. 'Lady' has a precise meaning and a considerable range of nuance in Nicholas's world, and he is using the word accurately.

Alwyn Forbes is said to have 'married beneath him' in *No Fond Return of Love*, a fact which is meant to be evidenced by his estranged wife Marjorie's vacuous mind, but is, in fact more forcibly validated by her 'mauve twin-set' and 'fluffy shoulder length hair.'

Jilly Cooper's upper-class character, Samantha, 'wears her hair long and straight and mousy...' (pg. 289) from which remark we can conclude, though it is never said, that as widespread and ordinary a custom as colouring one's hair, is considered, in that circle, vulgar. (L. *Vulgaris* — belonging to the common people)

Ironically, here in the United States, (where 'We the people' are the first words of the Preamble to our Constitution) the word 'common' is a positive one: the common good, the common defence, the common man,' et cetera. When Abraham Lincoln said,' God must love the common man. He made so many of them,' he set in motion a reverence for the quotidian that is still deeply ingrained in the American psyche today, over one-hundred and fifty years later. Most Americans, no matter what their income or status, refer to themselves as just an average American or a normal citizen or a common, ordinary guy. Kevin O'Keefe conducted a stunning study of this ingrained viewpoint in his highly lauded book, *The Average American*. (I think you would find it a fascinating contrast to Barbara Pym's world.)

In Jilly Cooper's book and in 'common parlance' among the higher classes in England, the word 'common' is always pejorative. It is used frequently throughout the text to mean coarse, vulgar, unseemly, gauche. As it is, though ambiguously, in Pym's work.

You remember earlier in our correspondence, that I wrote 'do not make the mistake of assuming that because we appear to understand our common language that we understand each other.' I think that you may begin to see that the use of that one word is (or at least has been) emblematic of one of our biggest differences.

In *The Sweet Dove Died*, which I am assuming you are reading now, you will come upon Leonora's reflection on her friend Meg's relationship with a very young man, Colin — such a common one, so unlike the exquisite rarefied liaison between herself and (the equally young) James.

You recall, of course, that Keith had a 'common little voice' in *A Glass of Blessings*, and that in *Jane and Prudence*, Fabian Driver, although not one of 'the villagers', was observed by the sharp-eyed Jessie Morrow from her window in this way:

> He looked just a little common in the grey suit, she thought; perhaps the colour was too light or there was something not quite the thing about the way it was cut. She could almost imagine that he might be wearing brown-and-white shoes, like the hero of a musical comedy in the twenties, but that was hardly possible. (JP pg. 191)

Throughout Barbara Pym's novels, certain kinds of clothes are common, (John Challow's shoes in *An Unsuitable Attachment* are 'a little too pointed — not quite what men one knew would wear,' pg. 49) as are accents, furnishings, teacups, topics of conversation, drinking habits, words, books, music, hair colour, mealtimes, etc. In short, an endless number of (mostly trivial) attributes can be, and are, evaluated and classified by the major and minor characters in these novels. But they are ranked ambiguously, enigmatically, cryptically, in phrases like 'not quite the thing...' as you have no doubt discovered. See if you can discover the relationship between these two quotations:

> 'His coming into the country at all, is a most insolent thing indeed, and I wonder how he could presume to do it. I pity you, Miss—, for this discovery of your favourite's guilt; but really, considering his descent, one could not expect much better.'

And:

> 'She didn't think she liked Mr— much. Of course one didn't want to be snobbish but it was really true that low origin betrayed itself somewhere.'

On the other hand, you will have discovered that little judgments exist everywhere. I doubt if you will find among your contemporaries anything as extensively petty as the rota of minute and intricate infractions prevalent in Miss Pym's world, but you will find them all the same. American branding/advertising depends on it.

But — I am extremely busy, and must stop here — we are in the midst of casting concerns — and I am needed. I will be unavailable tomorrow. The day after will be fine. Until then, why not think of what it might mean to be 'colourless/colorless and obscure.'

Yours—

Mallory Cooper

January 9, 2_____

Dear Felicity,

Please do not ask me about Hollywood. It will divert us from our purpose and I cannot possibly tell you what you want to know. And it is not glamorous. It is hard work. The glamour of Hollywood is one of our great American myths.

The reward is not the dazzle but the very basic satisfaction of the process. One has to want the process, not the end. I suppose I want this process, though god knows why. Too little sleep, too much schmooze, too many promises, too little fulfilment, too much travel, too little relaxation, too much wanting to be home, too much restlessness when one is home. Too much at stake, too little satisfaction in doing much else. The work is compelling. Making a movie — no matter what aspect of it falls under one's particular expertise, is an exhilarating creative process unlike any other. I feel extremely fortunate to be part of it, while keeping an ever-fading foot in the academy's door.

But Felicity, I don't think you know what you are describing by the use of the word 'Hollywood.' Yours is an outsider's perception of a very complex world, based on that small segment of it upon which its so-called reputation unfortunately rests. And yes, of course I know it is odd to be attached to both the literary and the entertainment worlds. But that is in fact my situation, and I am delighted with it. I too despise vulgarity, split-second emotions, crassness, and the urge to trample which you describe in other words as being characteristic of a society you have never experienced, in a business in which you have never worked, in a city to which you have never been. This is one of those 'assumptions' that we have discussed. And yes, at some (a few) media events, at certain parties, I look through the glamour at a throng of strained faces, which seem only to scan the crowd for opportunity, or look in the nearest

90

mirror. But that is not Hollywood. Or, it certainly is not most of it. There is no 'Hollywood' such as you describe. Most of the people who actually do the work in films are remarkably fine, extremely interesting, very talented and in some ways very ordinary people.

Hollywood's public reputation, was created by a media focussed on a small proportion of our more visible and ill-behaved actors, not by the writers, directors, producers, film editors, production designers, special effects people, camera people, costume designers, prop makers, caterers, drivers, stand-ins, extras, makeup artists, composers, arrangers, production managers, sound editors, stunt people, etc — 95% of whom are highly dedicated and talented people. They are family people, our friends and neighbours and colleagues, who go to PTA meetings and Little League games and dance recitals. True, they go in Malibu or Beverly Hills or Santa Monica or Brentwood or Pacific Palisades, but they go like any parent in Iowa or Wisconsin, because they love their sons and daughters like everyone else. This is the real Hollywood and, if I thought you were interested, I would tell you all about it. I suspect, though, that what you would like to hear about are the actors. But since nothing is more boring than talking about actors, except talking to them, let us proceed with our studies.

You have categorised several characters as 'dowdy spinsters':

1. Belinda Bede and her miscellaneous friends (STG)
2. Jane Cleveland, Miss Trapnell and Miss Clothier (JP)
3. Mildred Lathbury and her friends, Winifred and Dora (EW)
4. Dulcie Mainwairing (NFR)
5. Mary Beamish (GB)

They are indeed dowdy — some more than others — each more or less so in various circumstances. They are the mousy, neutral, camouflaged women of which we spoke.

Apart from the fact that Jane is not (technically) a spinster, Felicity — though I know what you mean — we do have a rather formidable frumpiness in this maidenly group. And yet, they are not destined to remain maidens. In fact, of the central characters you mention above; Belinda, Jane, Mildred, Dulcie, and Mary, only Belinda will remain single. As Prudence crossly observes to herself:

> Why couldn't she [Jane] have made some effort to change for dinner instead of appearing in the baggy-skirted grey flannel suit she had arrived in? Jane was really quite nice looking with her large grey eyes and short rough, curly hair, but her clothes were terrible. One could hardly blame people for classing all university women as frumps, thought Prudence, looking down the table at the odd garments and even odder wearers of them, the eager, unpainted faces, the wispy hair, the dowdy clothes; and yet — most most of them had married — that was the strange and disconcerting thing. (JP, pg.7)

To these we could add a host of others. I have just finished re-reading *Civil to Strangers and Other Writings*, a collection of Barbara Pym's unfinished and/or previously unpublished work (short stories, novels, novellas), which you really should attempt — in addition, of course, to the novels you have not yet read. It is stocked with prototypical or archetypal females. However, since you have finished the six you are obliged to read for your course, why did you make no reference to *Less Than Angels* in your list of dowdy spinsters?

You ask if it is possible to classify these variations as we did the men, i.e.

1. The Burdened
2. The Gracious
3. The Earnest
4. The Dull
5. The Husbands (in this case, Wives)
6. The Merry
7. The Ineffectual

Well, of course the women are burdened — this is what the novels are about — but their burdens are real ones: A distressing sense of inadequacy, frailty, guilt or debilitating loneliness. Serious burdens held within the heart, rather than those carefully constructed ones, handsomely displayed for admiration by Pym's men.

As for Gracious, Earnest, Dull, Spousal, Merry and Ineffectual — well, anything — anyone, can be labelled. But I think we cannot label these women.

This is the point, you see. This is what I have been trying to intimate with my brief remarks on bombs and ration books. And this is where the study of literature rears its beautiful head.

For however limited these women are within the fictional world, they are not, in our reality, flat characters. Unlike their male counterparts. They are round — spherical, planetary, inhabited little worlds 'made cunningly' in which so much of what they are is 'governed to the last fraction by the influence of their container...' and that container is their England.

Let us reach out in the dark to that fictional bedside table of Mildred Lathbury, and this time, let it be *Religio Medici* upon which the hand alights:

> We carry within us, [Sir Thomas wrote] the
> wonders we seek without us: there is all of
> Africa and her prodigies in us; we are that bold
> and adventurous piece of Nature, which he that
> studies wisely learns in a compendium what
> others labour at in a divided piece and endless
> volume. *(Religio Medici* in *Seventeenth Century
> Poetry and Prose*, Witherspoon & Warnke, ed.
> pg.336)

Or, to extend the Elizabethan context (and Donne's line), 'I
am a little world made cunningly/Of elements and an
angelic sprite...'

There is a short book, entitled *The Elizabethan World
Picture*, which you would do well to read. It is by E. M. W.
Tillyard, whose 'container' concept I quoted above and
whose work you will no doubt be required to read in your
Shakespeare or seventeenth-century literature classes,
should you decide to pursue your English studies. Elizabeth
I reigned primarily in the sixteenth century as I'm sure you
know, but the Elizabethan Age extended well into the reign
of James I, and is generally considered to be one of the
greatest literary periods in English history. Although all the
arts — including painting, music and architecture —
flourished during this eventful period, the pre-eminent
achievements were in literature.

The value of Tillyard to the study of Pym is the
intellectual/religious/social setting in which this belletristic
explosion took place, which is best summarised by the title
of his book, and best qualified by the idea of microcosmus,
a philosophy of a universal order, in which whatsoever is
bound on earth is bound in heaven — and the reverse. Or,
in other words, whatever order exists cosmically and
divinely, exists internally and morally and therefore,
politically and socially. This macrocosm /microcosm

doctrine was so intrinsic to the common assumptions of the day that, as Tillyard points out, few were moved to write about it.

Which puts me in mind of Isaac Asimov's *Robots of Dawn,* in which Elijah Baley, a private investigator of the future, must travel to a planet named Aurora, many light years from earth. En route, he endeavours to learn about the culture of Aurora by viewing 'book-films.' However, after countless hours of studying these book-films on every conceivable aspect of history, climate, culture, law, etc. and having made copious notes, he arrives at his destination, only to find himself lacking in the most basic information. He is frustrated in his investigations and confounded in both his private habits and his social relations by such practical considerations as how to operate the toilet — and the elaborate table etiquette of spicers, because it had not even occurred to the writers of informational book-films to address in their texts those things they held to be universal knowledge, based on universal assumptions.

In Elizabethan times, however, a few notable writers addressed the universal assumptions of their day — Francis Bacon, for one — and Sir Walter Ralegh, (yes that is the correct spelling) who, in his *History of the World* (1614) wrote that

> because in the little frame of man's body there is a representation of the Universal; and (by allusion) a kind of participation of all the parts there, therefore was man called Microcosmus...'
> (from *The History of the World* in *Seventeenth Century Poetry and Prose,* Witherspoon & Warnke, ed., pg. 26)

But you will have to spend some time with Ralegh yourself — and with Copernicus and his *De Revolutionibus Orbium Caelestium* (On the Revolutions of the Heavenly Spheres).

De Revolutionibus (1543) confronted Ptolemy's earth — centred, anthropocentric cosmology, which up until that moment, had been a universal assumption since the 2nd Century. And then came Kepler, Galileo, and Newton in rapid succession, all of whom threatened the very existence of the comfortable geocentricism from which Pym's favourite metaphysical poets sang like 'Air and Angels.'

But, never mind. You will already be growing restive and wondering what the point is. It is this:

There is a somewhat Elizabethan approach to village, neighbourhood, parish, and moral life in the novels you have read so far; an approach which has been described as 'tribal' by Tom Mallow in *Less Than Angels*, but, I think, is better described as a literary microcosm in which

> The heavens themselves, the planets, and
> > this centre
> Observe degree, priority and place,
> Insisture, course, proportion, season, form,
> Office, and custom, in all line of order...
> (Ulysses' speech, Act I, Scene III,
> *Troilus and Cressida*, William Shakespeare)

Not that Pym's characters hold Elizabethan views. Or not entirely. Rather, they hold their own views in the manner of their Elizabethan forebears; systematically, comfortably, safely — with about as much perspective on the distinction between their own few square miles of England and the rest of planet earth, as that of their progenitors four hundred years before, on the distinction between religion and science.

Although in their path from Elizabeth I to Elizabeth II, (with a brief stop in Netherton, perhaps, to change horses), the fictional and factual inhabitants of England have eliminated leeches and affixed television aerials, they remain essentially in the same place.

Such a place is the unnamed village of Harriet and Belinda Bede wherein it may even be an assumption 'universally acknowledged that a single man in possession of a good fortune must be in want of a wife.' (And no — I will not give you the source of that quotation — if you do not know it at this stage in your academic career, you should not be studying Barbara Pym.)

A very small piece of ivory indeed.

Until tomorrow.

MC

PS Yes, quite right — 'aspersion' comes from the Latin meaning 'to sprinkle' — although I like 'besprinkle' better, which is what my Latin books say.

There is a ritual in the Catholic and High Anglican Church which is called Asperges, whereby, in the principal Mass (or 'Service' in the Anglican Church) on Sundays during Lent, the Priest/Vicar/Rector sprinkles Holy Water on the congregation with an Aspergillum (sprinkler) all the while reciting Psalm 51: 'Asperges me, Domine, hyssopo...' 'Sprinkle me with a wand of hyssop, and I shall be washed clean, etc.' (In Paschaltide, this is replaced by the *Vidi Aquam*.) This ritual began to be incorporated into the liturgy on a regular basis in the ninth century, I believe. You will find it mentioned in *An Unsuitable Attachment*.

'Casting aspersions' really means conferring blessings, but over the years, it has come to mean that one has been judged to be in need of cleansing and has therefore been insulted. Interestingly, hyssop is one of the bitter herbs needed on the Seder Table for Passover — but that is a digression.

However, as I said before — no insult intended.

Mallory Cooper

January 9, 2_____

Dear Felicity,

A second quick note, before I am (justifiably) accused of generalisations myself. I am going on record here to say that my remark about actors was not all-inclusive. Nor entirely serious. It's a bit of a convention in our circle that most actors are extremely self-absorbed. Not all are, however and I/we respect serious, good actors and number several among our friends. It was also a reaction to the inevitable preoccupation of the public with what is on-screen as opposed to what (and who) is off it.

When you and I were discussing clothes, looks, Pym and academia, I said that I was not suggesting that you aspire to be dowdy so that other people would think you intelligent, because they would know it anyway as soon as you opened your mouth. You responded to that by saying that you understood what I meant and that you had always loved Helen Hunt's clever remark to Jack Nicholson in *As Good As It Gets*, which was: 'When I first saw you, I thought you were handsome. Then, of course, you spoke.'

I was going to let that slide, because I didn't want to be overbearing and you were just being colloquial. But Felicity, it wasn't Helen Hunt's remark. It was Mark Andrus' and James L. Brooks' remark. Or, within the fictional world they created, it was Carol Connelly's remark to Melvin Udall. Helen Hunt is a superb actress, beautifully talented. But again, just for the record, Andrus and Brooks wrote the words she spoke as the character they created. Every movie (like all the literature you read for your English degree) is, in its inception, a blank piece of paper. Until a writer writes on it, there is no character, no memorable line, and no actor. (No English Department either.) Remember that.

MC

January 10, 2_____

Dear Felicity,

You omitted *Less Than Angels* from your list because neither
Catherine nor Deirdre seemed to be dowdy spinsters? Come
now, Felicity, they are both unmarried, and Catherine has
been described as 'ragged' (pg. 7) and Deirdre's clothes as
'not particularly smart.' (pg. 22) They are therefore no less
spinsters, and no less dowdy than the others.

I suspect that you have omitted them for two reasons.
The first is that they are both young — Deirdre is your age,
in fact. The second is that 'ragged' and 'not particularly
smart' appear to be less pejorative terms than 'dowdy' and
are more currently in vogue (if the blue fingernails and
dung-coloured lipstick I see around campus are any
indication) than are 'dreary, dim and fawn-coloured.'

This book bores me far more than it does you. Not
because some of the characters aren't beautifully drawn —
but because they are. Malcolm and Bernard fill me with
dread. Together as one composite character, they represent
the greatest waste of time I have ever endured in real life —
a former suitor, whose unfortunate last name, 'Bend' so
typified his moral stance on anything, and who was so
fatuous and effete as to make Pym's men seem positively
virile, competent and fascinating by comparison that I find
it difficult to spend much time with them.

The narcotically dull suburban setting is so skilfully
drawn as to be an inducement to close the book and
Catherine and Deirdre are fairly flat characters — relatively
unformed and therefore uninteresting. As such, they can
engage neither a critical nor a general interest, though I may
be guilty here of too personal a response to the content of
the novel — a fault for which I once chastised you, I recall.
Still, although I have found considerable literary merit in
Miss Pym's portraits of suburban life — there are some

exquisite pieces — the novel seems to be a series of pieces — and I take issue with its somewhat slippery form.

We perhaps disagree about the relationship between form and content — me believing strongly that one is as important as the other — and you perhaps feeling, without really thinking about it, that the material content of anything is always more important than the packaging. Which, if drawn to its logical conclusion would mean that we appreciate the *Mona Lisa* because of its high quality paint.

Well, you seem to be taken with both the characters and the story in *Less Than Angels* — perhaps you will teach me something. One remark of yours I must address and that is that 'at least *Less Than Angels* is a love story — with real emotion and not just the remote love of God or church of some of Pym's other women,' who, you go on to say, are similarly remote in their love for men, whom they treat like little gods. All the women seem to do is 'wait and yearn and suffer'.

Well, but Felicity, our English word 'love' does not come from the Latin root — *Amor*, with its connotations of 'amorous' sexuality or at least romantic physicality, but from the word *lubet* — to please. In this way can one love a deity or another person — by pleasing him/her/it. (If one knew what pleased him/her/it.) Those who assume that keeping certain commandments will please God, try to do it. Those who believe that men are worth pleasing in a similar fashion, keep those commandments created by them. (Typing notes, correcting proofs — you remember Dulcie Mainwaring's list) Therefore love, in this sense, becomes an act of will, which (you are quite right) Pym's women tend to apply in all their relationships in lieu of wild acts of passion. They are mid-20th Century English gentlewomen, after all.

And that is not a disparaging remark — I do not say that they do not feel passion. I said that they tend not to act in such a manner — at least in public. We would be the first to complain if Belinda Bede suddenly flung herself into the

Archdeacon's bed. You and I — and he — would find it appalling, albeit for different reasons.

Far better to decide (to will) to do something, Miss Pym argues in her every page, than be propelled to do it, at least in most cases. Your 'Hollywood' does not agree with her, but all that undisciplined emotion on such large screens does get tiring. Which is why *The Sweet Dove Died* is truly a tragedy, and probably the only one that some minor studio would even consider making into a film. For about thirty seconds.

By the way, fear results in an act of will also. If one fears the consequences of not keeping religious or relationship commandments — hell, loneliness, social censure — (in Pym's novels, they are sometimes the same) one will keep them. Fearing or pleasing Setebos, (Read 'Caliban Upon Setebos', by Robert Browning when you can) are one and the same. Taken to extreme ends, Winston Smith ends up loving Big Brother, doesn't he?

Yearning is another and far more interesting matter. Ianthe's love for John is a case in point. The root of yearning has been traced to the Icelandic *girna* from *gjarn* which means both to be willing and to long for; while the root of suffering has been traced to the word fertile (from *ferre*, to bear or bring forth). It seems that we can bring forth our gods — divine or human — by being willing to suffer (as in sufferance — to tolerate, to <u>bear</u>) and longing, rather than love or fear. Interesting isn't it?

I really have not much to say about *Less than Angels*. I tend to agree with Robert Emmet Long, author of a critical work on Barbara Pym, who observes that

> *Less than Angels* is flawed... many of the characters are not filled in, and they seem to drift through the novel which, on the surface at least, lacks tension.
> (Robert Emmet Long, *Barbara Pym,* pg. 107)

But I am interested in your comments, particularly that 'everyone seems sad and funny at the same time', reflecting Catherine's comment that life goes on, 'comic and sad and indefinite.' When you have finished your seminar, perhaps you will let me know what your fellow students have to say about it.

Yours —
Mallory Cooper

PS I think if you look back you will see that I did not say that famous actors were 'ordinary people.' People who live extraordinary lives tend not to be ordinary. I said that most of the people who actually do the work in films are remarkably fine, extremely interesting, very talented and *in some ways* very ordinary people. I tend not to think of actors as the people who actually do the work in films (though that is unfair, I know) because they are the last ones in the process. Everything and everyone else — hundreds of people — are already in place by the time the actors begin their part of the work on a movie. But true — if in *some* ways they are very ordinary people, then clearly in other ways, they are not. Point taken.

January 15, 2_____

Dear Felicity,

I don't mean to be rude, but I am simply not interested in your experiences in self-help workshops. If you have a genuine question, I will try to answer it, but please don't send me your personal observations about group therapy. I detest those things.

As regards your poor roommate, I am delighted to hear that she has overcome a lifetime of feelings of inadequacy in one weekend. So would the Rosicrucians, and Dale Carnegie be delighted. These 'cures' are attributable to many causes.

But that vegetarian aromatherapy run-with-the-wolves mother-goddess tarot witchcraft cave-dwelling Berkeley navel-gazing is so old it stinks. Hundreds of my friends and acquaintances entered this fuzzy world of love, peace, ohm and grass, New Age Indian-Chinese, anything-but-European introspection vortex thirty-something years ago to 'deal with their pain' and 'approach their problems', hoping every day to emerge with the joy of having experienced a white light or the perfect moment. They still have all those problems and more!

And they are in the same stagnant state of perpetual self-analysis as they were in 1976. What your friend experienced seems to me to be momentary respite masquerading as enlightenment, and it will not work, except as bitter and short-lived entertainment. I can't believe a session would cost that much and produce so little. And you think Pym's women are dim?

Mallory Cooper

January 16, 2_____

Dear Felicity,

All right. *One* example. And then we must get back to
Tillyard. Yes, some of our friends are famous. And yes, I
have firsthand experience of the life they lead due to the
fact that I too live a similar life at times. Remember,
everything depends on the circle you live in. 'Famous', with
very rare exceptions, is a relative term.

   To answer another of your questions, no, I am not
famous, or even particularly well-known, but parts of my
life are or were attached to the genuinely well-known (some
of my books and other writing under a different name are
tied into the television and movie world and as such have a
crossover fan base) and my husband, in his heyday,
definitely was. He still is, in certain circles. Actors follow
him around because they want him to put them in a movie,
directors follow him around because they want work,
actresses follow him around because they can't help
following anyone male, handsome and powerful *and* able,
they think, to cast them in a production, and fans follow
him around because he was the producer of their favourite
show(s) some of which have an enormous following (I am
trying to be obscure here) and therefore he is a bit of a
demi-god. The on-screen people, as I have pointed out, are
the real gods to the fans. What does that mean? I don't
know. I don't think it means anything, really. 'Followers'
isn't a group I trust by definition and fans range from
judicious admirers to fanatics to the insane.

   And having said all this, most fame is confined within a
very small world. There are fandoms in every interest group.
If you went to the National Convention of Airplane Model
Makers, there would be geeks and enthusiasts and simply
talented people in that area who have their gods and heroes
and would come over and say to you in an awed voice,

'Look — my god — over there! That's Randall Gopherthorpe — he designed the 1958 Eco-Sunbird Mega-Sonic flyer. No glue! Can you believe it? I got one at auction by mortgaging my house. It has three SP-14 conklin-bats and a fortescue label. I'm not kidding. Forty-four stringlifters. I can't believe it. He's like my total f***ing hero. Do you think I could go over and talk to him? The autograph line is shorter now...' et cetera. (I just made that up. I don't know any Airplane Model Makers!)

So you could walk down the street in Topeka or New York (probably not LA) and see not one person on the street who recognizes my husband, but once you entered a particular circle of producers, directors, writers and executives or walked through the doors of certain studios, meetings, events, conventions or parties, it would be a whole other world.

If I told you his name (it is different from mine), it most likely would not ring any bells — but if you were in the entertainment industry and over a certain age, his name is a legendary one.

Back to your question about actors as friends. My closest friend was a well-known actress and yes, due to the fact that writers often have a little fame in some circle at some time in their lives and I wrote for her show (which is how we met), I had quite a following at one time. It was normal for several hundred to several thousand people to come to my talks and appearances. I had a small (and she had an enormous) fan club, we both had bodyguards at conventions, drivers and most of the paraphernalia that well known people have in this industry. Again, my degree of 'fame' was minor.

But really, there is no such thing as fame, Felicity, if fame means being known to a number of people. And it isn't all that much fun, no. Because fans are applauding and following an idea of a person and not a real person at all. These people have no idea who one is. How could they? As

I said to the aforementioned friend, (let's say her name is Ainsley, because it isn't) when she said dramatically, as was her wont, 'These wonderful, wonderful people (meaning fans) — look how they love me,' — 'Oh for heaven's sake, the only reason they think they love you is that they don't know you. They wouldn't put up with you for twenty minutes in real life — and you wouldn't tolerate them either.'

Believe me, it is true. We adored one another but she was an extremely eccentric and difficult person, always suing everyone, and very capricious. I am a certain kind of person and could deal with her. Anyone with a fan mentality would dissolve in an iconoclastic meltdown after a half-hour in the madhouse she calls home.

So yes, Felicity, the lives of famous people are different from those of the guy in the next office or the woman next door. Not intrinsically — not as human beings, but as people whose experiences differ greatly from others. 'Ordinary' — you are right — doesn't apply here. I tried once to explain to a relative why Ainsley (the two of us happened to be speakers at an event in the city near my aunt's home town) would not like to stay overnight at her house for 'a little home comfort' but I must confess that I did a bad job. I just said to my aunt that Ainsley would much rather stay at the hotel and so would I, given our schedule. And I promised to stay a couple of days with her after the event.

But my aunt was both hurt and bewildered. It seemed to her that her offer of dinner round the kitchen table with the kids and a night in her guest room was an attractive proposition. Or at least attractive enough to take Ainsley away from her quiet, elegant suite, her privacy, her haven away from people, her customary attendants, etc.

And of course my aunt did offer her home with a loving and warm heart. She was convinced in her own mind that my friend would truly enjoy a change — would feel happy to be in a warm and loving home, not in the 'fast lane' or the

106

'Hollywood set' or whatever inaccurate and outdated phrase she used and I could not explain why this was not so. After all, it's not that Ainsley did not have her own home, family and her own table. She was not in need an 'experience' of that kind.

And it wasn't that she was so spoiled as to require a massive amount of accoutrements every second of every day that would be lacking in my aunt's home. It's just that it would never have been an 'ordinary' evening at home with the kids. The conversation would have revolved around her for one thing. The dinner would have been beefed up a bit for company. And after a long day in front of thousands of people and signing hundreds of autographs and listening to everyone's favourite bit in their favourite movie or television episode, my aunt and her family would have just been more of the same:

'Remember in the episode about the tree falling on the roof? I loved that. You did such a great job. Didn't she do a great job, Bill?'

'What?' Bill says, tearing his eyes away from her for a second to plug in and to stop marveling that this amazing creature is actually sitting in his house at his table.

'I said didn't Miss X do a great job in that episode about the falling tree?'

'Oh. Yeah — uh yes, Miss X, you really did. But my favourite was the car episode — remember that? That was so funny. I remember the whole thing. Remember when Matthew Perry [or whomever] walked in the door and you already knew he was coming… that was great.'

'That wasn't the best one though, Dad,' one of the children breaks in, 'I like the one where you were walking on the roof. Of course I know you weren't walking on the roof really. How do they do that anyway? Was it special effects or did you walk on a like, low roof thingy or something?' This is after about eight hours of answering similar questions at the event.

'How do you like your coffee, Miss X?' Oh — strong! I hope it's strong enough. We would have got some stronger coffee if we knew you were coming. I hope this is okay. Jimmy, why don't you run down the corner to Safeway's and get some of that real strong coffee that Uncle Barry likes. You know the one with the red label — what? Oh, it's no trouble Miss X — Jimmy runs to the corner all the time, don't you, Jimmy, hon? Last week we forgot the butter and Angela's teacher was coming and...'

Compare that to a hotel suite alone or with me, her closest (and silent) friend, a movie in the room, a drink or two, dinner brought up to the sealed-off suite and the leisure to fall asleep in the middle of a sentence. Or compare it to getting together with some of one's fellow cast members and/or friends who are also attending the event, in the private hospitality suite next door just to sit and talk and laugh about things one has in common. And not to have to explain anything to total strangers.

Ordinary to Ainsley, and if I am honest, fairly ordinary to me, is the second scenario. And so, sometimes treating people as 'not ordinary' is the truer and much kinder thing to do. And that doesn't have anything to do with class or money or anything else. It has to do with work, with fatigue and with living the kind of life that is ordinary within a circle but not outside it.

It was the same in other worlds in which I have lived. The convent, for one. 'Ordinary' there can't even begin to be explained to anyone outside it. Little worlds are little worlds, no matter how big they are. And on this note, let us return to the Elizabethans.

Tomorrow.

MC

January 17, 2_____

Dear Felicity,

Thank you for the compliment but (and I mean this very, very kindly) never be in awe of anyone else's life. I know what you mean because I was once as young as you. I was, and am still delighted to be part of a very talented and dedicated group of professionals in which, of course, there are some demons, but also some near saints. But 'awesome' isn't the word to apply to this. What is awesome is what every woman can do with the life she is given, the choices she makes, and the path she creates. And everything comes with a price.

To return to Tillyard:

They (the Elizabethans) had in common a mass of basic assumptions about the world that they never disputed.Coming to the world picture itself, one can say dogmatically that it was still solidly theocentric, and that it was a simplified version of a much more complicated medieval picture.

Now the Middle Ages constructed their world picture from a conglomerate of Jewish and Greek thought, Plato's works and what you would call the Old Testament and what others (not having been convinced of the efficacy or even existence of a 'New' Testament) would more accurately call the Hebrew Bible. They were heavily influenced in this development by the newish Christian religion. This world picture resembled Platonism and other theocentric cults mainly in being perpetually preoccupied with the contradictory claims of two worlds—in this case, heaven and earth.

> ...the greatness of the Elizabethan Age was
> that it contained so much of the new without
> bursting the noble form of the old order...
> (*The Elizabethan World Picture*, Penguin ed. pg.
> 12)

The concept of macrocosm and microcosm is delineated
with clarity and grace in this short volume; although it is not
confined to the Elizabethans: we as a society are still
debating whether television represents current values or
creates them — whether in fact the fictional world creates or
reflects reality. In like manner, this kind of helical order
exists comfortably in the minds of most of Pym's central
characters, a good many of whom seem to be unusually
conversant with seventeenth century poets.

This is one reason we can legitimately ask: 'Is Pym a
twentieth century author?' It is also why, despite such
obvious flaws as her caricatures of men, a certain thinness
of plot, an occasional disregard of the passage of time and
perhaps too light a touch where it would be appropriate to
delve a bit, I feel we must consider Miss Pym's work
English literature.

Not, obviously, the greatest, nor the most profound; not
even, perhaps, 'quite the thing' as literature goes, but
certainly worthy of literary attention.

'The old truth that the greatest things in literature are the
most commonplace is quite borne out,' says Tillyard in his
epilogue. In this he is supported amiably by G.S. Fraser, the
notable Scottish critic, reviewer, and anthologist who says:

> The 1950s seem to me to have been a period
> particularly rich in novels which, without being
> wildly ambitious, hold one's attention by their
> general economy, intelligence and obviously
> accurate portrayal of some cross-section of
> contemporary life; the number of women

novelists whom one would like to deal with in a longer survey, Elizabeth Taylor, Barbara Pym, Elizabeth Montague, Penelope Mortimer, among others, is remarkably high. There are novels by women which can bog one down in the detail of tea-parties, babies' nappies or shopping expeditions, which can verge on the flavour of Mrs. Dale's Diary, and which can often shade off into an Angela Thirkellish defence of threatened gentilities, but which nevertheless often convey the texture of daily living, the drama of the undramatic, in a way most novels by men fail to do.

(*The Modern Writer and His World*, pg. 169-70)

I think we can agree, Felicity, that if Miss Pym's books are about anything, they are about the commonplace. And, since the commonplace is all that most of Pym's characters have, they are encouraged to make the most of it — by their church (the same church that was in full flower during the Elizabethan Age), by their society, their education and by their friends. Henry Hoccleve, in *Some Tame Gazelle*, is a representative of all four:

'I do so admire people who do obscure research,' said Belinda. 'I'm sure I wish I could.'

'Of course I have done a good deal of work on Middle English texts myself in the past,' said Agatha smiling.

'Now, Agatha, Belinda does not wish to be forced to admire you,' said the Archdeacon. 'After all, academic research is not everything. We must remember George Herbert's lines:

A servant with this clause
Makes drudgery divine,

111

Who sweeps a room as for Thy laws
Makes that and the action fine.
(*STG* pg. 68)

The next stanza of Herbert's (seventeenth-century) poem, 'The Elixir,' which is also the last, is really the *primum mobile* for Belinda Bede in this novel and for Mildred Lathbury, Dulcie Mainwaring and an assortment of lesser characters in her other works:

This is the famous stone
That turneth all to gold;
For that which God doth touch and own
Cannot for less be told.
(*Seventeenth Century Poetry & Prose*, Witherspoon & Warnke, pg. 859)

The stone to which Herbert refers in this poem is a religious metaphor for the secular 'philosopher's stone' also called the quintessence, or elixir, whereby base metals could be transmuted into gold by alchemists. And, by some accounts, eternal youth could be obtained. Alchemists were, of course, like most people who were not identical to their neighbours in the way the reigning powers wished them to be identical, originally persecuted in the Middle Ages. But they became almost respectable figures in Elizabethan Europe, not infrequently protected by kings, royals and aristocracy whose interest in keeping them safe was attached to their personal greed. Unfortunately, most alchemists who failed to produce the much-heralded gold to fill the royal coffers were summarily executed.

Still, the search itself produced some interesting by-products: a process for distilling wine was invented; Roger Bacon devised a recipe for gunpowder and directions for constructing a telescope; and Hennig Brandt, a respectable German scientist of the period, discovered phosphorus in

112

1669, while searching for the philosopher's stone. He obtained this from a residue of evaporated urine in the form of a white solid that glowed in the dark and ignited spontaneously upon contact with oxygen. 'Phosphorus' means 'light-bearing' in Greek. However, science progresses slowly and even in the early 18th century European apothecaries, in the pursuit of eternal youth, were still dispensing their *Elixir Universale,* a nauseating mixture of gold, powdered lion's heart, witch hazel, earthworms, dried human brain, and Egyptian onions, something I gleaned from a popular website (www.shvoong.com) though perhaps more respectably substantiated (without the specific ingredients) in *Alchemy in Popular Culture: Leonardo Fioravanti and the Search for the Philosopher's Stone* by William Eamon in the JSTOR volume, *Early Science and Medicine,* Vol. 5, No. 2, Alchemy and Hermeticism (2000), pp. 196-213.

Later in the 18th century, alchemists (chemists, by that time) while searching for the elusive elixir, discovered that scurvy could be treated with citrus fruit. They also discovered that foxgloves produced a chemical, digitalis, a derivation of which could be used to treat heart disease. The interesting thing is that by that time, the quest for youth and gold and glory itself had been transmuted into a pursuit of scientific knowledge for its own sake.

In like manner, any work, however humble, if undertaken for the glory of God, was believed to be transmuted into a noble act, deemed to produce considerable spiritual by-products: a sense of satisfaction in a job well done; a sense of microcosmic place in a vital macrocosmic undertaking, and an indefinable spiritual reward for not seeking attention or glory for oneself.

This belief has travelled unchanged down the centuries, in the Roman Catholic and therefore Anglican Church. Barbara Pym was certainly indoctrinated with it, as were the characters she created. Which is why, in Pym's work, we have to take minutiae seriously. It is also why we have to

113

take mousiness seriously — a fact you astutely recognised and questioned.

'Why would anyone make such an effort to maintain such obscurity?' you asked.

Because, Felicity, Barbara Pym's world is one in which obscurity in any form, including mousiness, represents a realm that you and I can scarcely comprehend, a legitimate cultural bequest — not only, as Jilly Cooper pointed out, from its ancient lineage of poets, scholars, nobles and kings, but also from the brave resistance and mutual support in a war we cannot remember; kindliness, modesty, and honour, free of the artifice of excessive 'personal enhancement' whereby a man or a woman, or even a book, may be judged by something other than its cover.

At best, the cultivation of mousiness is to participate in a distinctive moral past. At worst, it may indeed be a camouflage, brought about by war, under the protective covering of which the wish to inhabit one's own cosmos peaceably can be fulfilled.

And now — on to Tea.

Mallory Cooper

Tea

January 17, 2____

Dear Felicity,

I have been away from my desk for some time and have
only just received your email, in which you say your mind is
'a hodgepodge of poets, spaceships, vicars, wars, alchemy
and fawn-coloured underwear.' You have said in your past
correspondence that I 'seem to know so much about the
Church for a Jewish person.' Yesterday, you asked me how
'as a feminist, I could fail to appreciate value of women
helping women in empowerment workshops.' Indeed.

Perhaps you should have a cup of tea.
And while you are having it, ponder this:

I am not Jewish.
I am not a feminist.
And the hodgepodge is called 'education'.

Yours —

M Cooper

Dear Felicity,

I believe there is more imbibing of more kinds of liquids in *Excellent Women* than in any other of Pym's novels. The chief of these is, of course, tea. So much drinking of tea takes place that even Miss Pym gets tired of it.

> Perhaps there can be too much making of cups of tea, I thought, as I watched Miss Statham filling the heavy teapot... Did we really need a cup of tea? I even said as much to Miss Statham and she looked at me with a hurt, almost angry look, 'Do we need tea?' she echoed. 'But Miss Lathbury...' She sounded puzzled and distressed and I began to realise that my question had struck at something deep and fundamental. It was the kind of question that starts a landslide in the mind. (*EW*, pg. 227)

Ah — there seems to be another email from you in my inbox. I shall retrieve it.

'Please can we talk about what you said about emotion in your email, before we go on to tea?' you request. You also say that your 'philosophy of life' is one of 'feeling and emotion,' which is what drew you to English Literature in the first place, and you wish I would appreciate that—you find it difficult to deal with me sometimes. I am cryptic. I expect too much. I seem to be more sensitive to the feelings of the characters in the novels than I am to yours and you would like to know why.

All right.

First of all, if you look back over our correspondence, you will see that you make a good number of assumptions, not unlike many of the characters in Miss Pym's novels.

The difference is that they have some basis for their assumptions, having lived in their world for many, many years with people of similar if not identical viewpoints on almost all fundamental issues. They have just cause, as it were, to assume. And when they don't, they are misled, as you sometimes are.

Now, I have said that I study with a Rabbi and that my husband and I had guests for the second night of Chanukah. I have mentioned the Kabbalah and the Seder table. I have said that I am not a Christian. You, therefore, have assumed two things. One is reasonable; the other is not. The first is that I am Jewish, which is reasonable, though incorrect. The second is that Jewish people do not know about the Church, which is neither reasonable nor correct.

First of all, I study with a Rabbi because I want to. No other reason. His first language is Hebrew; his second, Yiddish; his third, Aramaic; his fourth, Russian; his fifth, English. As his English is not only flawless, but inspired, I can only assume that his other language skills are impeccable. (A reasonable assumption, since he has been published in four of his five languages.) I like to be able to understand the origins of scriptural texts — I am deeply interested in the origins of the laws, canons and assumptions of Western Civilisation and therefore I study with him. He has a doctorate in philosophy, and one in Hebrew Letters and since I am doing research in literary philosophy, he is an invaluable source of help to me. But more than that, Felicity, we are friends. He is both brilliant and loving — a deep and elevated soul.

In fact, as I believe I indicated more than once in our earliest correspondence (I don't know how you could have missed my references to the convent) I am Catholic by birth — or baptism if you prefer. An old Catholic. One of the disdainful, predatory, aesthetic, ascetic, disagreeable types. Taught by Augustinians, Benedictines, Jesuits. Fluent in

117

Latin by age seven, capable of grilling oral exams in logic at age eleven. Not particularly interested in content; adamant about form. Hard ethics. Dismissive of dogma, sceptical about 'social issues.' Four degrees. One in Theology.

I have said 'I am not a "Christian".' Insofar as I understand *your* use of the word, that is true — I did enclose it in quotation marks and you did tell me in your Christmas email that you 'went to Baptist services on Christmas morning' and nothing can be further (in the Western tradition of religion) from my spiritual psyche than that. Can assumptions be made about this? Maybe. I doubt they would be accurate. Let me offer you a quotation, by way of an answer. I suspect you will not understand it, but it's the best I can do:

> Leonie propped her chin on her rake.
> 'I'd never advise anyone to become a Catholic,' she said. 'If you're one, you've got to be one. But you can't change people. Catholicism isn't a religion. It's a nationality.'
> 'It's funny, Leo,' mused Nanda. 'You say the most extraordinary things; you're awfully slack about prayers and all that, you've even got a copy of Candide bound up as a missal, and I believe the nuns know, and yet you get away with everything. Yet if I do the slightest thing, I'm punished.'
> 'Because they're not sure of you yet. You're a nicely washed and combed and baptised and confirmed little heathen, but you're a heathen all the same. But they're sure of me. In ten, twenty years, I'll be exactly the same. It's in the blood. I'd as soon be a Hottentot as be anything but a Catholic. It may be nonsense but it's the sort of nonsense I happen to like…'
> (Antonia White, *Frost in May*, pg. 122)

The conversation above, as you may have gathered, takes place between two (twelve-year-old) children—one, Leonie, from a 'very old and very wealthy family whose name, to Catholic ears, had something of the glamour of Medici or Gonzaga…' and the other, Nanda, a recent convert, from a Protestant family. It is preceded by another, perhaps more illuminating, exchange, an excerpt of which I think I should include here. It begins with Leonie:

'Do you really believe all the things in the catechism, for example?'

'Why, of course.'

'You mean you want to believe them? Being a convert, you have to make an effort… more than I, for example. And so you come to believe them better than I.'

'But don't you…'

'Believe them? I don't know. They're too much a part of me. I shall never get away from them. I don't want to even. The Catholic Church suits me much too well. But it's fun to see what a little needle point the whole thing rests on.'

Nanda's world was spinning round her.

'Leonie, what on earth do you mean?'

'Well, for example, there's no rational proof of the existence of God. Oh, I know there are four the Jesuits give you. But not one that would really hold water for a philosopher.'

'But, Leonie, that's sheer blasphemy,' said Nanda stoutly.

'Not necessarily. It doesn't affect the goodness of the beliefs one way or the other. After all, there's no rational proof that you exist yourself.'

This had never occurred to Nanda. For quite fifty yards she walked in deep thought. Then she burst out:

'Good heavens… it's quite true. There isn't. Leonie, how awful.'

'I think it's rather amusing,' said Leonie, beginning to whistle. (Pg. 81)

There are a great many Catholics out there who would dispute this. But most educated Catholics of my generation would not. And we have far, far more in common with educated Jews (who by the way are enormously well-versed in most of the broader, and a surprising amount of the finer, points of Christianity) than we do with Baptists. (Which incidentally is why both religions are considered equally un-Christian by hard-core fundamentalists) I'm not talking about minor ideological differences — 'The Messiah has come'/'The Messiah hasn't come.' The fact that both agree that there is a Messiah and that his arrival is/was expected is a far more important issue. Not that I believe in a Messiah — or rather a messianic person. I believe in redemption of other kinds. You will argue here, perhaps, that Baptists also believe in a Messiah. True. But it is the meaning of 'belief' that counts here — *credo quia absurdum* and all that — in which disbelief is incorporated into a belief system; and the way, in which symbolism replaces literalism that binds these two branches of the same tree together. I'm talking here about a species of being, a bloodline perhaps — a common ancient, internal language.

But never mind.

The simple fact is that my husband is Jewish, and I, once a Benedictine nun, am not. However, this is not the place to discuss these things. Suffice to say that were an elderly Rabbi, an elderly Jesuit, and an elderly Fundamentalist Baptist Minister to sit in a room together, neither of the first two would be the odd man out. As for the recent born-again hysteria that has gripped this nation, I have no I idea what, or even if, they think.

Second: Your philosophy, you say, is one of '...feeling and emotion.' Do they differ? And even if they do, I'm not sure that philosophy incorporates either, its chief distinction from the passions being reason. Perhaps it would be more accurate to say that philosophy recognises the validity of emotion in a relationship between one entity and another — in this case, I am assuming, between the student and her subject. Or, as you seem to intimate, between the tutor and the tutored.

Well, Felicity, I hope you will not take amiss the fact that emotion has little to do with this correspondence. Or rather, despite any feeling that may arise, the chief of which has been, so far, irritation on your part, my sole object is to help prepare you for the kind of rational thinking that you will need in order to succeed at Yarmouth.

Third, since you will not be judged on what you feel about me or my philosophy — or, in fact, about Barbara Pym's work, but only on the reasons you give for feeling it, you must begin to examine your assumptions and measure them against a larger reality. Has it not occurred to you that those very feelings and emotions could be holding you back? That every assumption you make based on personal reaction or meagre information narrows your path — or misdirects you onto a less than useful one?

This does not mean, as I have said before, that you are expected to have no emotion about what you read, what you think, what you experience — of course you are — but it does mean that any conclusion you draw from it has to be based on something other than that emotion (or supposition) in order to be of value to you in your studies.

It also means that the topics we have discussed bear further examination. There may be legitimate feelings, other than those immediately discernible to you, for the pursuit of Alwyn Forbes; the darning of the Archdeacon's sock; the

121

helpless, tragic, descent into emotional slavery of the middle-aged Leonora for the young, beautiful, homosexual James. And you may dispute those feelings. No one says you have to agree with them, but you have to: a) know what they are, and b) have a convincing reason for doing so.

Why? 'Because the old truth that the greatest things in literature are the most commonplace is quite borne out'— and that being the case, they are common to you and to me.

Perhaps you would consider enlarging your philosophy. Those feelings, of which you are so aware, may be better employed under the guidance of reason than in its stead.

Apply them to poor Connie Aspinall who must now go to Africa and sleep with Bishop Grote; or to Mark Ainger, who must compete for his wife's affections with a cat, just as you might apply them to your ill-used roommate and her callous boyfriend, or the sad sweet child in your Sunday school classroom whose only friend is his dog. Their motivations in seeking affection or acceptance are no different.

I want you to feel — and feel deeply about literature. But I also want you to know why and how these emotions are engendered by the writer, the text (apart from the writer) the words (apart from the text) as well as the relationship between the reader and all of the above. I also want you to be able to take that emotion out of any equation when it is necessary to do so. Otherwise, we could all take courses in 'My Favourite Books' and spend endless and idle time in a group resembling your friend's therapy session 'sharing' our feelings about why we just love *Gone With The Wind* and how cool *Harry Potter* is. Not that there is anything wrong with that, intrinsically. But it's not what we do in academic literary studies. If that's what you want to do, join a book club.

In any case, it is not the province of philosophy to incorporate emotion, only to recognise it as a co-relative path to the same truth.

Do not forget that in this correspondence we are talking about Barbara Pym's world in which we find that there is often something slightly sinister about emotion — something 'not quite the thing' about a willingness to turn the head just a little too far toward its object. It is that Elizabethan conceit again (conceit in this context referring to its original definition as an idea or notion — and later as a fanciful idea or notion) of intentional balance, personal and universal, so that not even peripheral perspective is lost. For what is gained in the attempt to stray too far from an established centre may be only some faint misinformation about reality. Or so it seems, does it not, in these decorous works? You might like to explore that in your new essay.

Perhaps what you meant to describe as elemental to your philosophy is intuition (*tueri, tuitus.* Latin: to protect; intuition; to look upon, to guard), which is not as far removed from experience as one might suppose. Intuition is pre-experience — truth already looked upon, and not recognised until crude empiricism confirms it. And, it has served you well to date. Your instinctive response to *Some Tame Gazelle* was incisive. You 'had a feeling about it' which in itself is an experience of that thing. You extended your own experience of estrangement into an English morning circa 1935, smelled the dead chrysanthemums, and 'something quivered.' Something you couldn't define, you said. But you can. You will.

And although true knowledge is said to be grounded in the empirical, we really cannot eliminate the indefinable as having been experienced. (Although, in the study of literature, one must certainly try to shed some light on it.) Critics in general tend to deny the inexpressible as unworthy of having been genuinely encountered. But I do not think that this 'looking upon' with inward eyes, should be regarded as any less of an experience than a 'looking upon' with its ocular counterpart.

Ouspensky, in his *In Search of the Miraculous*, categorises four states of consciousness as being available to humans: Sleep, waking, self-remembering and objective. The first two are ordinary, unremarkable, functionary states. The third is what distinguishes man from beasts, and the fourth is 'clear consciousness' — seeing things as they are, un-correlative to subjective experience. Usually experienced by most people only in 'flashes', this property, Ouspensky states, is a product of not identifying with oneself—not even calling oneself by the pronoun 'I.'

I think this last property or quality is most advantageous in the study of literature. The other three will always be with us. They are what unites us under the canopy of the 'commonplace.' But the fourth — to see an act purely, or a Mildred Lathbury clearly — without reference to oneself, is what allows us to penetrate that canopy and illuminate it. It is this quality of perception that allows one to appreciate the fact that the significance of a caterpillar in the cauliflower to Miss Prior may be equal to or greater than a rejection of proffered friendship to oneself.

Finally: Surely you understand by now that when I say that I am not a feminist, I mean that I am not *merely* a feminist. I am not definable by that term, because I am not primarily interested in the plight of women. Neither am I primarily interested in the plight of men. Nor am I *primarily* interested in African Americans, Hispanics, Whites, Asians, or any other artificial division of the human adult world, though I am *inclusively* interested in all of it. These adults can take care of their own plights. I am primarily interested in the plight of children, all of them, male and female, who cannot. Hence the value of education. And that is enough for one day.

Mallory Cooper

January 19, 2_____

Dear Felicity,

'The novels are awash with, they are inundated with tea.' So says Charles Burkhart in his delightful *The Pleasure of Miss Pym*. On the surface, he appears to be correct — tea does seem to be rather a preoccupation in Pym's novels. In fact, it is not. Or rather, although it is more predominant in her works, it is no more significant than it is in many other English novels.

Consider the opening of *Portrait of a Lady*: 'Under certain circumstances there are few hours in life more agreeable than the hour dedicated to the ceremony known as afternoon tea.' Henry James, of course, was not English, but this sentiment certainly is — although few Englishmen (or women) would say 'afternoon tea.' At least, not in England. (Although it is permissible to write it, if necessary.) I have never heard any English person use that phrase, other than one particularly pretentious ex-patriot at a university press, who, his colleague once remarked to me, (quoting Jilly *Cooper*) 'had every pseudo-refinement of the lower middle classes.'

Of course, Americans and a few stray Canadians I have known use the phrase 'afternoon tea' since, of necessity, it must describe verbally what the English understand culturally. And yes, there are various kinds of repasts known as tea, but it is understood, from whom the invitation comes, what form 'tea' will take. If a member of the upper middle or upper classes were to invite you to tea, for example, it would be understood that he or she meant tea in the afternoon and not dinner or supper. Speaking of which you may have noticed that in *An Unsuitable Attachment*, Sophia chooses her words carefully when calling on Ianthe in the evening.

'We do hope you've finished your supper — dinner,' said Sophia, uncertain what form Ianthe's evening meal might have taken.

'And that you aren't in the middle of watching your favourite television program,' said Mark conscientiously, for his parochial visiting now made this question automatic.

'I have finished my supper and I haven't got a television set,' said Ianthe smiling. 'How nice of you to come.' (*UA*, pg. 31)

The number of subtleties in the little scene above is fascinating. Sophia and Mark, although they have done some preliminary classification by noting; a) the fact that Ianthe had been in church regularly since she moved to the neighbourhood; b) her family background (a canon's daughter) and; c) her appearance on the street in what seemed to be a chinchilla coat, are nevertheless cautious about assuming that she is a person 'of one's own kind.'

However, she has had supper rather than dinner at this hour, thus blurring the lines of demarcation a bit. The definition of dinner, once the ceremonial glittering evening feast of the upper classes, diminished after the war to mean simply 'the main meal of the day' whenever it took place, though traces of its original glory remain in some circles.

At one time, (and to some extent, today) the 'working classes' had their primary meal in the middle of the day, and a high or meat tea as soon as the breadwinner(s) returned from work — at what was by other classes considered to be an unfashionably early hour. The upper or 'leisured' classes, not having a work schedule per se, had lunch (at which 'no gentleman ever took soup') around one, tea at four-ish and dinner at about eight, or even nine. The children would have had their main meal at lunchtime, tea at four and a very light supper before bed, since: a) they did not eat with the adults and, b) it was thought to be (and is) healthier for children not to eat a heavy meal before going to sleep.

As this was generally understood in Barbara Pym's world, the point of such delicate enquiry on Sophia's part can only be surmised. One explanation is that when in doubt, or times of transition, the English often revert to Nursery habits. And, since children in traditional upper class households had dinner at noon and a light supper sometime between afternoon tea and bedtime, Ianthe's consumption of supper in the evening is able to be interpreted by a member of her class in a variety of ways.

In any event, Sophia and Mark would have calculated Ianthe's social stratum on the basis of other factors — the furniture and general decor of the room, the kinds of books on the shelves (and the fact that there were books on the shelves). A thousand little things, none of them articulated, including the fact that Ianthe offered them coffee instead of tea after dinner/supper, would have determined in which way the Aingers would interpret 'supper' and conclude, as Mark did, that Ianthe was a 'very obvious gentlewoman.' Consider this little exchange in *Jane and Prudence*:

'I suppose we could give Mr. Lomax tea, though it wouldn't be quite the usual thing. I wonder if we are well-bred enough or eccentric enough to carry off an unusual thing like that, giving tea after a meal rather than coffee? I wouldn't like him to think that we were condescending to him because his church is not as ancient as ours.'

'Of course coffee does tend to keep one awake,' said Nicholas rather inconsequentially. (*JP*, pg. 16)

No one but an English person could have uttered those words. They appear to be contradictory, as it is understood that the well-bred thing is to have coffee after dinner.

But if one is well-bred enough, you see, then these wild eccentricities are possible, and can be attributed to superior social liberties, in-breeding of the upper classes or some such other justification. On the other hand, the main point of the quotation above really has to do with the classification of churches, and not tea at all.

Belinda Bede does invite her friends to a 'supper party' in the pre-War *Some Tame Gazelle*, but that is to indicate the type of food (cold with a hot soup preceding it) and the fact that the guests need not wear dinner jackets. (There is, of course, no tea.) Besides, it was a Sunday, the midday meal of which, Sunday Lunch, had, and has still, somewhat sacramental properties. One cannot have Sunday Lunch at dinner time. Moreover, the clergy had been invited.

This English Sunday lunch has been described by social psychologists as a symbol of security. The security of the home, and of parental affection, is symbolised in home cooking (Mother's cooking is always the best) Family ties continue to be powerful in England... many families never miss Sunday lunch reunion...

> A joint of beef is usually roasted with its attendant circle of potatoes in the roasting pan, for roast potatoes, like Yorkshire pudding, are an integral part of the meal. So are the other accompaniments — mustard; snow-white and fluffy horseradish sauce; a boat of rich, brown, hot gravy. Green vegetables, perhaps some carrots, add a splash of bright colour to the harmony of pinks and browns on the plate...
>
> A fairly generous amount has been prepared, for second and third helpings are usually expected, in spite of the knowledge that

a large and sugary plum pie must surely follow, crowned with thick cream. How formidable! How delicious!

[The Englishman's] taste is formed today, as it has been for centuries, in the nursery and the school dining room. The childish habits remain with us and now the middle-aged schoolboy enjoys his habitual meals in the club dining room or the factory canteen...

Our taste for such food is ingrained. The dishes our mothers cooked for us, we in turn cook for our children, a practice that ensures the survival of a national cuisine. Strange, is it not, how so many of us yearn for the foods on which we were nurtured? An Englishman spends half his life in the jungles of Africa, and dreams of a steak and kidney pudding, followed by a jam sponge and custard. (*The Cooking of the British Isles*, pp. 59-60; 154-5)

Let us put this to the test, and look in on the Bede household, Harriet, Belinda and their maid, Emily, on the day that their supper party is to be held:

The day had begun as other Sundays did. After breakfast, Belinda had consulted with Emily about the roast beef, and together they had decided what time it ought to be put into the oven and how long it ought to stay there. The vegetables — celery and roast potatoes — were agreed upon, and the pudding — a plum tart — chosen. In addition, the chickens for the supper party were to be put on to boil and Emily was to start making the trifle if she had time. The jellies had been made on Saturday and were now sitting in the cool of the cellar.

> Belinda had suggested that they might have a
> lighter luncheon than usual, as there was so
> much to do, but Harriet was not going to be
> cheated out of her Sunday roast... (*STG*, pg.
> 103)

You see, Felicity, there are so many, many intricacies
involving the diaphanous but immutable definitions of class,
all of which incorporate a serious measure of security,
(safety, silliness) — in the form of food, mealtimes,
television programmes, soap animals, a bowl of quinces,
Asperges, frozen vegetables, George Herbert, et cetera, that
they are impossible to define here. Or anywhere, really.
Because, quite likely, The Bedes' maid, Emily, and her
parents, brothers and sisters would have been sitting down
to an identical Sunday Lunch, as would Lady Clara Boulding
who had opened the bazaar the Bedes attended a few weeks
before. There would be a thousand differences in that
identical ritual and yet no one would or could explain them.
Either one knows them or one does not.

Actually, Jean-Pierre le Rossignol attempts an
anthropological study of the English Sunday Lunch in *Less
Than Angels*, you remember, but anyone who is ignorant
enough to sit in the Dulkes's pew in church ('...such a thing
had not happened to the Dulkes in all their forty years at the
church') even though there is no real reserving of pews
allowed, will not be able to ascertain the little gradations
involved in what he calls 'the traditional English Sunday
dinner with joint.' As indeed he is not. He goes to his
meeting in Bayswater — 'a message from the Other Side,' he
explains — as uninformed after his experimental meal as he
was before.

An old refrain has been bouncing through my head
apropos this silent dominion of social distinction, but I
don't know where it came from or who wrote it. However
here it is — it may amuse you:

In telegraphic sentences,
half nodded to their friends,
They hint a matter's inwardness—
and there the matter ends,
And while the Celt is talking
from Valencia to Kirkwall
The English — ah the English—
don't say anything at all.

'A matter's inwardness.' That is the mini *vade mecum* of Barbara Pym's novels. All of them. All of them. There — I have given you an invaluable tool to take into your seminar next week. You must do what you can to employ it.

This ragbag of quotations that opens from time to time in my mind contains such treasures. Of course, they would be more valuable if identified, which I am normally able to do. It gives you the opportunity to go to the source, and me the ability to ascertain how accurately I have cited. This time, however, I'm just not sure. It does sound like Kipling or Stevenson, though.

Well, to return to the main subject, tea is a fairly standard class indicator. Those who are not part of English culture by nationality or experience, often mistakenly use the term 'high tea' to refer to a dainty après-midi collation. In fact, nothing could be farther from the truth. 'High tea', also called 'meat tea' as I mentioned above, is a substantial evening meal served with innumerable cups of strong, sweet, Ceylon tea. It is a 'working class' tea, if you like, with the kinds of foods common to this group. It is called high because it is consumed at a 'high' or dining table as opposed to a 'low' tea (or coffee) table. Or as Jilly Cooper puts it:

On to tea which for the unwary is also full of pitfalls. It is very common to call it 'afternoon tea' to distinguish it from 'high tea'. The upper classes drink China tea out of China teacups...

131

the lower classes Indian tea which they drink
very strong and very sweet. (*Class*, Jilly Cooper,
pp 266-67)

Ms. Cooper goes on to point out a previously infallible class
criterion that I have found to be very much still in effect:

Now that people of all classes use teabags,
everyone puts the milk in second, so this is no
longer an upper class indicator.

In fact, our dear Dr. Hall, Oxonian that he is, has always
posed the question, milk jug poised over the empty cups,
'Are you a pre-lactarian, my dear, or post?'

And tea leaves (as opposed to bags) are still doing a brisk
business at the culinary establishments I frequent. In any
case, returning to Ianthe Broome, we know as readers
(because we have been informed in the paragraphs before
Sophia arrives) what Sophia surmised by instinct — namely
that Ianthe's supper, a proper one, did not include tea:

Ianthe was not the type to pour herself a glass
of sherry or gin as soon as she got home after a
day's work, nor yet to make a cup of tea. One
did not make tea at half past six in the evening
like 'the working classes', as her mother would
have called them. Instead she set about cooking
herself a suitable supper in the almost too
perfect little kitchen. The grill was heated for a
chop, tomatoes were cut up, and a small packet
of frozen peas tipped out of its wrapping into a
saucepan. 'We have come to this,' her mother
used to say, 'eating frozen vegetables like
Americans.' She had been deeply conscious of
her position as a canon's widow. (*UA* pp 30-
31)

132

Now, one could look at the fact that traditionally, even as late as 1963 when *An Unsuitable Attachment* was written, truly upper-middle to upper-class women normally did not go out to work at a salaried job (thus depriving someone more needy) every day. Nor did they usually have to cook for themselves. An old-fashioned, single woman like Ianthe would have been among those who, like Mildred Lathbury or Dulcie Mainwaring, simply did volunteer or church work. But that is a nicety that Barbara Pym explains simply by saying that 'When her father died, it had been necessary for her to do some kind of work...' though of what that necessity consisted, she does not say. One doubts that it was financial, since Ianthe, who 'had never been in the position of having to wait until pay-day,' is able to buy a house, fly off to Rome without consulting her pocket book, and generally to acquire violets and sherry and chicken breasts in aspic without any thought of cost.

The point is that there are a number of seemingly irrelevant and random factors upon which the delicate structure of class is built, the least of which is income, and the greatest of which may be, in addition to a slightly too pointed shoe, a cup of tea.

Is this all rather silly? Yes. But the English are silly. As I have said before, silliness is their salvation. You made another (understandable) assumption a few weeks back, Felicity, when I said to you of the English, 'Besides, I think they're silly.' You wrote back, 'Why did you stay in an English environment and study English literature for so long, if you think they're so silly?' I did not answer that question because I thought it would become apparent. My statement to you was: 'I respond positively to aggressiveness, innovation, practicality, and improvement to a degree unintelligible to the English, and which, if it were, would be abhorrent to them anyway. Besides, I think they're silly.'

The Old English meaning of silly, which you will find still in common use in Elizabethan literature, is 'happy'. And I meant to use the word in two ways. As an American — I think it would have been silly, in the colloquial sense, not to change the spelling of 'Tunbridge', which is next to Tunbridge Wells, to 'Tonbridge' if that change makes life run more efficiently. It seems a sensible choice not to have your Visa bills misdirected, returned, delivered late, paid therefore late, incur a late charge and the wrath of the Credit Bureau. But that is a silliness that would apply if those towns were in the United States (with the exception of a few oddball counties in New England). And it is a silliness that I cannot employ in the life I lead.

However, in the England in which I lived years ago and in Pym's England, that silliness ensures that whatever is worth all this trouble (to them) remains safe — a town, a land, a people, a civilisation — a microcosm. To incorporate American methods or characteristics (aggressiveness, innovation, practicality, and improvement) into that world, however admirably they operate in ours, is a mistake, on a local scale, anyway. In this, the English are — well, English. I think they should be left, as should all cultures, to live their lives the way they choose. This is why, in reading Barbara Pym whose observations of her own era, culture and class are as keen as though she were not an integral part of it, our world is expanded, not narrowed, as many people think. It might as well be another planet, one whose vices (if that is not too strong a word) are initially more apparent than its virtues, as you have come to see. I know this is not a full answer to your question. But this is much too long now — and tea deserves more attention. Let me continue tomorrow, when I have finished our screenings.

MC—
PS. I got your email entitled 'Confidential' first thing this morning. You're welcome.

January 20, 2_____

Dear Felicity,

No, I don't think that anything you end up knowing will be as a result of my having 'stuffed you with my education.' That isn't, in fact, possible, education being the extraction of what is already within one: from the Latin to 'bring out' (ducere: to lead). From the same root as 'duct', which in the case of teaching would be appropriate, allowing for the possibility of mutuality if we add 'con' to it. Conductions are made both ways. Interestingly, Duke is also from the same root, meaning a leader. Se-duce, to lead astray, in-duce, to lead or bring in, pro-duce, to bring forward. My object is merely to induce you to produce. Fascinating, isn't it?

Don't worry about it. You will see that I have given you so little information relative to what is needed, that you will spend your course frantically ploughing through what resources you can find, in order to learn more and more, and to keep yourself safe. Yes, safe. 'A little learning,' as you know, is a very dangerous thing...

M. Cooper—

Oh yes. Pre-lactarian. Why?

January 21, 2_____

Dear Felicity,

A river of tea flows through English literature with the serenity of a summer afternoon — sometimes in a stately manner, as in *Portrait of a Lady* (which is in fact American Literature though it claims literary kinship with its forebears) at other times simple, even meagre. But it is always there.

It represents different things of course. Virginia Woolf's Helen Ambrose, 'over two dishes of yellow cake and smooth bread and butter', cries out with manic energy: 'You look ill!... Come and have some tea.'(*The Voyage Out*)

Somerset Maugham reveals a young man's class and his impoverished circumstances, in entertaining (well, seducing really) an older woman.

> On the table was a plate of cakes and two cups, a sugar basin and a milk-jug. The crockery was of the cheapest sort... he came in with the tea in a brown pot. She ate a square sponge cake with pink icing. That was a thing she had not done for years. The Ceylon tea, very strong, with milk and sugar in it, took her back to days she thought she had forgotten.' (*Theatre*, Penguin, pg. 84)

Rebecca West's description is more dramatic.

> 'Come, my love, let me put a well-fed cushion beneath your head. Are you better now?'
> But her upward smile, though she nodded, was still some way from perfect serenity.

'Ah, I have it!' he exclaimed. 'You feel the need of tea. Is it not so? I had forgotten the dependence of your sex on tea!'

'Ah, yes,' breathed Harriet meekly, 'you are always right. I am feeling the need of tea!' (*Harriet Hume*, Virago, pg. 133)

Barbara Pym's characters (both male and female) often feel the need of tea. In fact, among the few passions (if they can be so described) she does portray, the craving for tea is among the strongest. 'How I long for a cup of tea,' Ianthe exclaimed within minutes of arriving in Rome (Rome!) for the first time.

'Well, we're just going to have one,' said Penelope, thinking how typical it was that Ianthe should long for such a dull and essentially English thing as a cup of tea. She hardly liked to admit that she wanted one herself. (*UA*, pg. 145)

It is difficult to over-estimate the importance of tea in these novels, if not England. Notwithstanding its precipitous symbolism in the Revolutionary War (still referred to in some parts of England as the 'American Rebellion'), where else would tea be considered a good enough reason to officially interrupt a ball game? Not just a cup of tea — but Tea. The real thing: Biscuits (cookies), cakes, scones, sandwiches, tarts, etc. It's almost worth enduring an interminable cricket game, just to enjoy the tea.

'The British population buys about 500 million pounds of tea a year', according to a note I once made on an old recipe card for Dundee cake. Odd, the notes we make. I can't imagine having wanted to know that. However, it may be useful if only to emphasise how great the consumption of tea is. And how much greater it must be now — that recipe must be ten or fifteen years old.

There are many kinds of tea, each with its attendant status — unblended teas like Assam and Darjeeling from India; Ceylon (now Sri Lanka) teas, which are smooth and fragrant; and Keemun, or English Breakfast tea, a black tea from China. The more popular teas are blended teas, like the Irish or English or Scottish or Welsh mixtures of Sri Lankan, Kenyan and Chinese teas. I order various teas, blended and unblended from various estates around the world, through a company called Upton Tea Imports, one of the most courteous and efficient companies with which it has been my pleasure to interact. Entering their website is entering an enchanted tea-world. I think it would both charm and educate you and I urge you to browse their pages for a taste of the civility that was once the hallmark of the finest purveyors of commodities so aptly illustrated in Barbara Pym's novels. However, this is a huge subject and one that I suggest we take up privately if you are interested, once we have examined its significance in Barbara Pym's novels. Upton Tea Imports can be found at www.uptontea.com

It may interest you to know that although tea has been a part of English life since 1662 when Charles II married Catherine of Braganza, from Portugal, where tea was already a fashionable drink, the 'tea table' per se came into its own only in the eighteenth century, when the Duchess of Bedford turned it into a feminine soirée. At that time, and in that place, the gap between lunch and dinner had been growing larger, so that too many hours of ennui stretched between one culinary gathering and another.

Breakfast, for the upper classes, was really a man's meal. Few women of the gentry or aristocracy appeared in public in the morning. Therefore, the pleasures of the tea table at four were very welcome, and thus began a ritual that endures to this day. And it *is* a ritual, however casual it may seem at times. All sorts of things are done. And not done. It is not rigidly ceremonial, (the food varies slightly, as does the setting) but it does have definite unwritten rules.

I have attended more, and hosted more, teas than any other social event in England and Canada, and can attest to the fact that they all have had in common one thing of which Matthew Arnold would have approved: Sweetness and Light. The fare being sweet, and the conversation, light. Not that I approve of Matthew Arnold, with his disgraceful attitude toward the Welsh. Wretched little xenophobe. But he does write well.

Conversation at teatime is significant in that it must be pleasant. Even before the advent of the refinements of the Duchess, this was understood. When in 1710 or so, Joseph Addison collaborated with Sir Richard Steele to lighten and improve the art of essay writing in *The Tatler*, his aim, he said, was to bring philosophy out of the library and 'lead her to the tea table.'

Or, as that same cookbook puts it:

> Afternoon tea is not a time for discussion of matters of state unless perhaps the vicar or the lone male who happens to be unoccupied in the afternoon wishes to deliver a weighty opinion or two; the talk is indeed of the garden or of the vicar's trouble in repainting the vestry.
> (*The Cooking of the British Isles,* pg 42)

This cookbook wasn't written in the Victorian age—it was written in 1971, when *Dirty Harry* and *A Clockwork Orange* came out; Georgia O'Keeffe's *Black Rock with Red* was exhibited; Mariner 6 went into orbit around Mars, Saddam Hussein took over Iraq; John Lennon's album, *Imagine* was released; Bangladesh became an independent nation and *Ms.* Magazine was launched.

Still, the conversations — and I remember them — were only about such topics as schools, children, gardens, cooking, cultural events and clothes. No matter who was there. Had Ms. O'Keeffe or Ms. Steinem been present, she would have had to comply.

Anachronistic? Yes, of course. That is the purpose, the consequence, the benison, the meaning of tea. What it was in 1740, it is now. And when the bombs were falling over England in 1940, I am absolutely positive that someone made tea, and everyone talked, for a few minutes, about bottling gooseberries.

Yours
—*Mallory Cooper*

January 22, 2_____

Dear Felicity,

No, I don't think we should meet before your course begins next week, even though you are nearby. And on that note, there can be no correspondence between us on this subject after your course begins. Your lecturer must be your sole source of contact about your course material and requirements after that. As for help with literary theory, I assume you jest. Apart from my aversion to the subject, I have been scrupulous in avoiding any reference to theorists or those critics currently in vogue in academia throughout our communication.

You must find your own voice first. And then, if you find affinity in a theorist's views or a critic's stance, employ their work to buttress yours. Or, perhaps to change your mind.

Few of the authors I suggested you read (other than the references within the novels) will stand you in good stead in your coursework. The only thing they will do is enable you to appreciate a world that is gone — the world of which Barbara Pym was an intimate part — and to help answer a question you never asked of yourself: why you signed up for such a course in the first place.

You won't endear yourself to your professors by adopting my viewpoint, nor do I think you have it. One of the reasons that Dr. Hall sent you to me is that he thought you were an exceptional person — someone who will one day make a mark in the literary world. That being the case, and I do not disagree with him, let me remind you that the hallmark of an independent scholar or writer is to depart from the norm, not to adhere to or hide in it. But for the time being, you are in university to learn what you will one day take exception to — as well as to learn what is meaningful, enriching and worthy of further pursuit.

Let me, then, offer you a menu, rather than any specific suggestion:

You will be, if you have not already been, exposed to a number of literary philosophies. They will seem confusing at times, brilliant at others, nonsensical, overblown, fascinating, repellent, familiar and ridiculous. They will also seem stimulating, dull, compelling, astute, delightful, simplistic, contorted, complex, one-dimensional and insane. That is because they are all of these things and more.

Therefore, I fail to see how anyone can be an adherent of any of these critical paths exclusively. Moreover, it seems positively backward to think that it is appropriate to examine every text with the same methodology. My colleague and friend Peter Miles, the former head of an English department to which I was years ago loosely appended, thinks I am being as dogmatic in my aversion to theory as the theorists are about their own pet labyrinths. On the other hand, he says, 'I could happily agree that it is the sign of a closed mind to believe that one methodology will elicit all that might meaningfully be said about a text; I too tend towards eclecticism — but I have no hesitation whatsoever in applying my own particular favoured methodology to all the texts that I encounter in expectation of it producing the best insights. However, in doing so, while I delight in the fruits of that particular methodology, I will also become wryly aware of further things that are worth saying about the text but which are *not* to be framed within the terms of my favoured methodology. And so I remain eclectic.'

To my mind, this is a wise and admirable educator. I wish there were more of him.

Diagnostics differ, Felicity. Not that literature is a disease, although literary activity has been called a 'contagious mental illness' by the Turkish philosopher, Baha Tevfik, and as you know, English literature definitely was not considered a subject worth studying until the

142

nineteenth century. But if you are going to diagnose a text by which I mean identify the nature of it (or its problem/theorem) by its symptoms (signs, symbols), which is certainly what we do in academic courses, then it would be wise for you to have a look at the theories that abound.

I will give you a list of those of my acquaintance with my brief and cranky comments (do not take these to heart) and you must research them for yourself.

Historicism: Core idea: *What really happened?* Purports that to understand a text, one must understand the author's biography and socio-cultural background. It is comparative in nature and brings other disciplines to bear upon the text. Major flaw in my estimation is that it eliminates transcendence, the pure idea, the madness of poets and a book like Einstein's Dreams.

Structuralism: Core idea: *Basically, there is no author. Not really.* The truth (whatever this is) has already written by the time the un-author puts pen to paper and therefore he or she is irrelevant. Clearly would appear to come out of cloud cuckoo-land at first glance, until one happens upon the very splendid and very pure linguistic philosophy of Saussure. As a scholar, I find this core idea brilliantly credible; as a writer, insulting; as a reader, inconsequential.

New Criticism. Core idea: *Both writer <u>and</u> reader are irrelevant.* (I didn't make this up.) This theory reveres text and pretty much text alone. The words. It explores the relationship(s) between form and content — between what and how something is said in the text. What the author intends or the reader perceives is discounted — which, if pursued to its logical conclusion, makes one wonder how the critics' own reading of a text is relevant. Or their writing about it. Still, to be fair and respectful to the great minds attached to this line of criticism, I have to say that the word itself, divorced from its creator and its reader, is worth examining philosophically, linguistically, scrupulously, closely. Not much to do with reading actual books, however.

Archetypal: Core idea: *Literature conforms to a tribal consciousness or archetypal memory.* Individual works are created/determined by an innate impetus to manifest the larger human drama rather than tell an individual story. I don't have a quarrel with this, essentially, and as I am so fond of Northrop Frye's *Educated Imagination* and *Anatomy of Criticism,* will only say again that it is counterproductive to wisdom and understanding to examine anything from merely one point of view. This viewpoint, in practice, is less guilty of this infraction than most.

Psychoanalytic: Core idea: *Literary work is a neurotic manifestation of an author's disordered psyche.* Okay. Well, not much to write about here. Hopefully you will find some merit in this approach to literature and tell someone (preferably not me) about it one day.

Feminist: Core idea: *Women's writing has been devalued and underrepresented in literary tradition and women as characters have been extremely poorly and inaccurately portrayed in literature by patriarchy and phallocentricity of men.* There is little to which one could object in this historically verifiable viewpoint, except to say that this theory is fragmented by those who fiercely believe that women are a separate literary species whose thinking and writing is an entirely separate branch of literature (*écriture feminine*) and those who believe that both men and women are legitimate proponents of feminist thought. The drawbacks are the usual — the inability as a result of this thinking to see anything else — or to see it in other than a confrontational light. Again, the danger of dismissing a range or even an aspect of alternative literary thought because it may not fit into the theory rears its mean

144

little head. However I cannot overemphasize the benefit to the literary world that resulted from this movement: the resurrection and proliferation of outstanding women's literature. Two sources of such treasure are Persephone Books and Virago Press. I think you would find them sources of inestimable value.

Marxist Core idea: *Literature is a social/political institution in which class struggle is not only a fundamental component but also an ideological mission.* Well. Marx appeared to believe in the autonomy of art, but his followers certainly do not. The pro in my view is that Marxists are blessedly concerned with content and are thus empathetic with the ambition or mission of most writers, which is actually to say something. Con — I cannot think that literature itself is an institution, even if institutions have sprung up to imprison it. Art is not an institution. But, that's just me...

Cultural Core idea: *If it is traditional, classic, 'high-brow' and/or established, no matter what its intrinsic value, we oppose it.* These are the people who write PhD theses on *I Love Lucy*. What they say is that they examine, elevate and/or rescue marginalized or oppressed art, artifacts and cultures, but I think they just like watching reruns. Essentially it is an anti-white European male movement. As I happen to like white European males or rather their writing (though clearly not exclusively and, as clearly, very selectively) I find it a little pointless. You don't have to be opposed to something just because you want to do something else. But, again, I'm not the best person to advise you on these things. I wrote a (very well-reviewed) book on the philosophy of *Star Trek* for a prestigious university press. Still, I'd never submit it as a serious qualification for an English degree.

Poststructuralism Core Idea: I don't know what the core idea of Poststructuralism is, since one of its fundamental

145

properties is that no text has a core. I shall rely on you to inform me one day. What I do know is that it is multifaceted, multi-layered, complex and has elegant components. Although eschewing oppositional relationships, it is itself dialectic, hermetically binary — from Barthes' meta-language/ language and readerly/ writerly postulations to Kristeva's normal/poetic, semiotic/orderly, fluid/fixed equations.

At its heart is deconstruction, which is founded on the belief that no text is stable but is rather a set of deep contradictions, that are internally opposed to itself. Intriguing for an intellectual mind, sufficiently obfuscatory for an academic mind, and injurious to a creative one (at least prior to or while creating).

Postcolonialism/Postmodernism: Core idea: *If it is traditional, classic, high-brow and/or established, it has probably had enough attention so we examine and give credence to genuinely marginalized art, artifacts and cultures.* These divisions of literary theory are actually distinct but they overlap and they all have to do with power – dominant cultures as opposed to alienated or Third World cultures and/or peoples. It runs the risk, as most counter-movements do, of devaluing what was formerly considered to be significant (and often still is) by aggressively or disproportionately lauding what is significant to them and disparaging all else. Also elevates relatively unchallenged material to 'classic' status. Seems a little bitchy from the little reading I have done. Also naive.

New Historicism: Core idea: *Literature is a product of an historical setting in which there is an indivisible connection between a text and the culture of an historical period.* These critics focus on discovering (or possibly creating) an inter-textual historical narrative — a specific paradigm of contextual authority. Tillyard and his *Elizabethan World Picture* is an example of one kind of New Historicism though there is wide variance within this theory as the definition of history (the occurrence of actual events as opposed to the retrospective narrative about them) is disputed. It seems to me reasonable that most artists are connected to the times and places in which they live, but it is also reasonable to explore the ways in which they might not be.

I was not sure what I thought about the New Historicists except that they did not seem to depart from the old Historicists as much as they would probably like. But my PhD supervisor once sent me a polished note about the 'detection of absences' which I love. 'One of [this theory's] key themes or approaches' he wrote, 'Is the detection of 'absences' and the significance of those absences or what is held in abeyance. This approach can easily be made to sound absurd, but handled well it can be quite suggestive.' I was always surprised and delighted by the way he could elicit some measure of fascination from me, by simultaneously polarizing and connecting the essential components of reasonable theory. He passed on a valuable quotation from New Historicist Paul Strohm, a former professor in the Faculty of English at Oxford, which I now pass on to you:

> 'My quest is not only for what a text intends to say about itself but for those moments of inadvertency or lessened vigilance when it means more than it says.' (*England's Empty Throne*, New Haven and London: Yale University Press, (1998), p. xiii).

'Lessened vigilance' is something you might want to consider in the interpretation of Barbara Pym's work, Felicity. It has something to do with that intuition in which you have such faith, and which has served you well in your reading thus far.

Reader-Response: Core Idea: *Literature is empirical and therefore it is the experience of reading it that constitutes its meaning.* Essentially, the reader is part of a jolly two-person team and co-creates meaning with the author as s/he reads. Reader-response theory examines the series of interpretations and reactions the reader experiences in her/his interaction with the text. The trouble with this is that there are intelligent and/or informed readers and there are stupid and/or ill prepared readers for every given text. I don't see how everyone is equally empowered to contribute to the meaning of the text. Nor do I give credence to the presumption that a reader knows more (or even anything) about what the writer intended than the writer him/herself but again, this is something for you to discover if you are interested. I'm not, very.

Finally, the basic relationship of one theory to another can most effectively be summarized by Professor Quincy Adams Wagstaff, President of Huxley College:

I don't know what they have to say,
It makes no difference anyway,
Whatever it is, I'm against it.
No matter what it is or who commenced it,
I'm against it.

Professor Wagstaff is played by Groucho Marx in *Horse Feathers*, 1932 (Paramount Pictures). The song 'I'm Against It' (music by Harry Ruby and lyrics by Bert Kalmar) was performed by Groucho Marx. The fact that he is wearing academic regalia while singing it is a nice touch.

However, you might want to have a look at Professor John Lye's superb Brock University website for some rather more practical assistance. It can be found at http://www.brocku.ca/english/jlye/literary-theory.php

I think you will find it enlightening.

148

Now, where is your essay?

Mallory Cooper

PS I read an article in the *New York Times* a few years ago
about a literary critic who had come to the conclusion that
no one has to actually read books at all. One just needs to
read criticism and theory. Rather like the old imperialist
conclusion of the Catholic Church not to allow people to
read the Bible but only the commentaries on it provided by
theologians (like *they* have a clue about moral and ethical
principles in real life.) I don't think this professor has been
banished to a bookless netherworld (yet) but I am sure
some fervent librarian is on the case. If not, I volunteer.

January 22, 2_____

Dear Felicity,

I think you know the answer to that question. I do value universities, I do value scholars, I do value intellectuals, I do value literary analysts and I do value some academics. In fact, I cherish all of these in principle (and at times in reality) deeply — much more than you could possibly know. That is why I detest the mean, petty, inadequate and phony versions of all of these things. I don't want you to be in awe of the wrong people, listen too closely to the wrong voices and learn the wrong lessons. I don't want you to waste your young life unlearning what has harmed you. I want you to study everything you can with a protective shield called 'perspective' and this is what you will acquire by self-education. Learn *about* literature from every professor you have. But learn what it means from yourself. And the only way you can do this is to read, read, read.

'What if you read Balzac's Lost Illusions,' writes my esteemed colleague, Elif Batuman*, 'and, instead of moving to New York, living in a garret, self-publishing your poetry, writing book reviews, and having love affairs — instead of living your own version of Lost Illusions, in order to someday write the same novel for 21st-century America — what if instead you went to Balzac's house and Madame Hanska's estate, read every word he ever wrote, dug up every last thing you could about him — and then started writing?'*

Dr. Batuman, who has been described as having 'the wild soul ...of an academic,' is the sort of professor I described in our earlier correspondence – emblematic of the kind of teacher you must seek out. And while I would object to the impression in that wonderful description above which implies that academics universally have wild souls, for you have seen that they most certainly do not, you must find those who do. If you read her book, *The Possessed: Adventures with Russian Books and the People Who Read Them,* which I suggest you do, you will find the reference above and also permanent value.

Now, I am pleased that you have been finding our interaction so useful. I think, however, although I thank you for your comments, that this is more to do with you than me. I did tell you that if you read these works with care you would find something 'relevant' in them.

And no, I certainly will not give you one of the lectures that I deliver on Barbara Pym. You are entering another professor's class next week. That would be unethical. Besides, this is my research, and my work. You must do your own. I do, however, understand why you asked and what you need, so I propose a compromise. Let me give you an outline — just an outline — not the entire content — of one of the lectures I have given on *Jane Eyre*. You will be able to extrapolate useful bits relative to Barbara Pym from this.

When I start my seminars, Felicity, I tell my students what we will have attempted to accomplish by the end of them.

For my last seminar on *Jane Eyre*, (quoting from my lecture notes) this was the goal:

By the end of the week we will have explored and hopefully answered these questions:

1. What are the major and minor themes in this novel?
2. Who are these 'book people' – these Brontës?
3. What are some traditional critical viewpoints on Charlotte Brontë and *Jane Eyre*:
4. What are some contemporary critical viewpoints on Charlotte Brontë and *Jane Eyre*?
5. Why anyone should read *Jane Eyre* today? Or in more academic terms — what is the significance of the novel?
6. How might we, with ensuing aesthetic and intellectual satisfaction, approach the examination

of the text. Or in more humble, and to my mind more appropriate words, 'How should we come to this book? What should we respectfully bring?'

We will ramble among the following in our effort to answer these questions:

Feminist theory. The Marxist response to this novel — this political, social, economic and class-conscious *cri de coeur.* Victorian values. The Chartists and electoral Reform. Anger, Passion, Bunyan, Byron, Mrs. Sarah Stickney Ellis. Locations. Angels. Names in the Novel. David Lodge's excellent essay on Jane Eyre entitled 'Fire and Eyre'. Mastery and Slavery issues. The rhetoric of power and — who cares?

Then Felicity, I said something like this (again, these were just notes; I have tried to fill them out a little for you):

Let me start off for the benefit of the three people in this room who may not know this: I have no great love of literary theory. Nor of literary criticism since 1980 or so. When I was a contributing editor to Arts and Letters Daily, the managing editor used to hold an International Bad Writing Contest every year — and it was invariably won by academics.

Apropos of this, I was, at the time, a scholarly editor at a prominent university press, employed, paid (and paid well) to quietly rewrite academic books because they were so badly written, so unnecessarily convoluted in such appalling English, that they had to be translated from university-speak into intelligent English so that the press would have at least a chance of selling more than three copies.

When my husband votes for the academy awards, he votes from among five choices in most categories: there are just under six thousand members of the Academy of Motion Picture Arts and Sciences. From that number, a series of committees is formed each autumn. Those who will choose the five nominees for best actor are actors (actor-members of the Academy). They will screen all eligible films and will in the end vote for the five of their choice. Those five names are submitted to the entire body of Academy members who will then vote from among them. Hence the best actor to whom an Oscar will be given at the Academy Awards Ceremony has been selected initially by a jury, so to speak — a judging committee of his peers.

The same goes for directors, costume designers, art directors, producers, music, special effects, and much more, including writers. *Writers.* Why? Because the Academy has ruled that anyone who is not a proven writer and/or has not been or is not now successfully writing, has no business judging the excellence of writers. Only writers select the five best scripts for award consideration.

Why then, should it be any different in an academic (as opposed to an arts) academy? Why would those who could not write a *Jane Eyre*, or a book of similar quality of any kind, or a work of lesser quality — or any novel at all (and who, when they do write books of criticism, write them so badly that they have to be entirely re-written by an actual writer), feel entitled to criticise those who do? Critics without qualifications cannot be taken seriously.

Now to the whole truth: a certain entitlement is conferred on those who are not writers but who are gifted with insight — who read beautifully, read with understanding, penetration, grace. This is not common, but it does exist. Sometime next year I have a book coming out which some kind scholarly reviewer has called a 'graceful series of elucidations.' I hope that praise is deserved but whether it is or not, it is a worthy goal to attempt. What I respect, what I would have you practice, is literary analysis — an incisive, yes, but respectful exploration of the word and how it is employed, communicated and understood in a text and the ability to articulate it. A graceful elucidation. Not a hatchet job.

So — let us look at this book, this *Jane Eyre* — *with* the best of our analytical properties and the whole of our respect.

Here are the six questions again. (Felicity, these are mere scraps of what ensued in the classroom. Just notes of mine which set off discussions among the seminar students — but as notes, they may be useful to you in your similar exploration of Barbara Pym.)

1. What are the major and minor themes of this book?

    The Role of Women and its attendant concerns of Duty, of Sacrifice. Power and Imprisonment – from the first page of the book – to the last – when some of the power issues in Jane's life are resolved because of the change in Rochester. So of course, then, Justice. Religion. Anger. Imprisonment for Charlotte Brontë (for all three sisters) the imprisonment of the soul on the earth. Love. Transcendence. Largely transcendence. How all these things co-exist in a person whose society says she may not have most of them.

Again, my view, not unsupported by others, is that this is a religious work, though contemporary criticism would have it opposite. It is easy to see why. Religion and society were mutually dependent in a way that we cannot dream of in western civilization these days. What offended the state offended God and vice versa and Charlotte Brontë was nothing if not offensive. Her religion was not an established one — though she tried, via Helen Burns, via St. John Rivers, via her own uneasy conviction that Bunyan was right. She takes aim against him, as does George Eliot in Mr. Bulstrode (and as does Dickens in any number of

154

characters) but in the end, she constructs a pilgrimage for Jane — just like Bunyan's *Pilgrim's Progress*.

One of the major themes of *Jane Eyre* is the construction of a viable religious sensibility, which went through several stages — denial/rejection of the Brocklehurst version of 'Christianity', a wistful periphery with regard to Helen's saintliness — for although Jane recognizes Helen's peace of mind, her nature prevents her from being able to subscribe to it. Her later sheer abandonment of herself to the power of love begins to make sense of virtue/faith before she falls into a dichotomy of denial of another kind in giving up Mr Rochester. This is synthesis — a forging of one's own instinctive beliefs with one's taught beliefs — and finally an emergence of the soul in its return to the object of its desire on its own hard won terms. That is the bildungsroman thread. Jane essentially is a character slightly apart from this action. Her attention is captured by her social condition while the religious drama she incorporates is played out internally.

Which brings us to the second point:

2. Who are these Brontës? Very briefly, they are wild-eyed motherless children, Branwell, Charlotte, Emily and Anne whose older sisters Maria and Elizabeth died in and from the damp cold cruel malnourishment of Cowan Bridge school to which the four eldest girls (Anne remained home, being too young) were sent by their father. This father, Patrick Brunty, from Ireland had changed his name to Brontë (meaning in Greek 'thunder') and, surprisingly, expected his children to know the crucial issues of the day and to debate them with originality. After their mother had died, he brought his surviving daughters home, where, united in grief and isolated in the parsonage at Haworth in Yorkshire (set bleakly and dramatically in the moors

as though a tornado like that in the Wizard of Oz had dropped it in among the windswept heather), the children constructed an elaborate fantasy life. They created worlds, which they called Angria and Gondal — finely-wrought microcosms of society, complete with laws and systems and values and moral adventures, echoes of which haunt (and convictions from which impregnate) the later works of all three sisters.

3. What are some traditional critical viewpoints on Charlotte Brontë and *Jane Eyre*? [Here, Felicity, I have omitted a very long history lesson about the Chartists and the Electoral Reform issues of the day.]

4. What are some contemporary critical viewpoints on *Jane Eyre*?

[And here, Felicity, I have omitted another long section of notes about the status of women in Charlotte Brontë's era and her reaction to it, which brought us to Charlotte's overriding passion in all her novels: social reform particularly as regards women. And that brought us to feminist criticism.]

5. Why should we read Jane Eyre today?

Because we are still interested in the issues raised in her story:

Patriarchy, morality, anger, justice, religion. The need to be loved versus the need to do the right thing for oneself, whatever that right thing is seen to be. The need to create legislature that is inclusive — and to repeal that which is not. The thin wavering line between who I am and who you are. The limits of our abilities to accept the limits of the society we need if we do not fit easily into it or if there is no place for us.

In addition to these issues, we read it for its impassioned, if at times graceless, prose, its wish for transcendence, its parallel to earlier moral works — its incorporation of several literary traditions:

> The Gothic in form
> The Bildungsroman in intent — or in consequence.
> The Romantic in sentiment.
> The Religious in import.

Why do we read *Jane Eyre*?

We read it for its life-affirming passionate intensity, for the way in which fiction addresses fact, for the imaginative wedding of the four traditions above. We read it for its well-formed plot — for its engagement with its reader — that factor I called 'a terrific story.' We read it for its influence on later literature and for its manifestation of the literature that came before it and, conversely, its reliance on a tradition of prose and poetry that we too examine from our difference stance — our own little brief span on the planet. We read it for its profound characterization whether we think these characters are themselves profound or not — and whether we like them or not. We read it for its connection to other writers.

Felicity, here there is a long passage about the Byronic hero and Childe Harold and Charlotte Brontë's preoccupation with Byron. This is not relevant to your purpose so I have omitted it. However, with regard to Pym and her men, none of them are in the least Byronic. Consequently they are hardly redeemable, being unaware of themselves (and therefore their flaws) and the wider world (therefore immune to comparison and censure). They are needy, however, and so you may want to consider my conclusion:

157

My thought is that the central attraction of the Byronic hero is that he is both redeemable and needy. In need of a good woman. In need of oneself, in fact, dear Reader. Which in Rochester's case is expressed explicitly in what has often been said to be one of the most famous romantic passages in all of literature:

> I sometimes have a queer feeling with regard to you — especially when you are near to me, as now: it is as if I have a string somewhere under my left ribs, tightly and inextricably knotted to a similar string situated in the corresponding quarter of your little frame. And if that boisterous Channel, and two hundred miles or so of land, come broad between us, I am afraid that cord of communion will be snapped; and then I've a nervous notion I should take to bleeding inwardly.

Harold Bloom notes that 'between them, the Brontës can be said to have invented a relatively new genre, a kind of northern romance, deeply influenced both by Byron's poetry and by his myth and personality, but going back also…to the Gothic novel and to the Elizabethan drama.'

Like all of Charlotte's characters, Rochester is a psychologically profound creation, intricately crafted and just enigmatic enough to have kept literary debate alive over a century and a half — and another reason for reading this book. So now we have some reasons. Students must find others (or delve more deeply into the ones discussed in the seminar) about which to write essays or exams.

6. How do we approach this book — what do we respectfully bring? We do not bring an untrained mind. We do not bring inexperience to bear on art. We bring our best perceptions

158

cultivated by the widest knowledge we can glean about the writer's world, her literary history, his personal history. But more importantly, we bring appreciative intelligence — not the wish to destroy but the wish to evaluate meaning, find significance — moral , political, aesthetic, feminist, historical, cultural. We bring an informed consciousness. We inhabit the imaginative and literary world of the writer. Not just this specific writer, but the writerly mind — the impetus, the act. We bring a knowledge of what the best minds have brought to bear on this work — particularly the aesthetically gifted, the literarily endowed, the beautifully educated, the clerisy, you.

We read it from within.

[In this vein, Felicity, see if you can pick up a copy of Francine Prose's superb *Reading Like a Writer*. I think she will answer more of your questions than I.]

Mallory Cooper

PS By the way, the most interesting result of this lecture came from an aside. I had discovered that one of the critics I read in preparation for this lecture remarked that Jane Eyre had the best depiction of 'cold' in all of English Literature, quoting a passage about the schoolgirls walking back to Lowood from church on a winter Sunday. I thought that that was a nonsensical pronouncement. So I dove (dived!) deep into my literary memory and my books and found a half dozen or so descriptions of cold in literature across the centuries. At the end of the lecture, I read both the critic's remark and the passage from *Jane Eyre* aloud. And then I read passages from Keats' sumptuous 'Eve of St Agnes' with its benumbed beadsman, and Virginia Woolf's *Orlando*, in which the Thames froze and life upon it was magic, and A.S. Byatt's short story, 'Cold' from her collection entitled *Elementals,* (an entire mesmerizing story about the nature and effects of cold) and Shakespeare's bare, ruined choirs, where late the sweet birds sang. And then I went on to talk about the value of having the (or a) history of English Literature in one's head.

This is when the students became most animated. In fact they became deeply involved in the pursuit of depictions of cold in literature across the centuries — coming to see me for days afterward with bits out of Jack London (who of course was American but who certainly wrote about cold with flair) and more Shakespeare and Tolstoy. Someone brought in 'The Wanderer' and I believe another typed up a bit of Dickens and put it in my mailbox. Dylan Thomas, Dostoyevsky, Joyce, Eliot, Blake, Whitman, Tennyson, Shakespeare, Lawrence, Emerson, Blake, Nashe, and dozens more. I still have a little box full of literary cold. This is what engaged them, this pursuit of comparison, this voyage into interconnectedness, this quest after cold. This algid, arctic, benumbed, biting, bitter, blasting, bleak, boreal, brisk, brumal, chilled, crisp, cutting, ectothermic, frigid, frigorific, frore, frosty, frozen, gelid, glacial, hawkish, haematocryal, hibernal, frost-bitten, hyemal, hyperborean, icy, icebox, intense, keen, nipping, numbing, penetrating, piercing, polar, raw, rimy, severe, sharp, shivery, sleety, snappy, snowy, stinging, Siberian, wintry literature — all of it — infused them with fire, for days.

January 23, 2_____

My dear Felicity,

I cannot say that the improved quality of (the first page of) your essay surprised me but the degree of its excellence did. This is really exceptionally well done. You must show it to Dr. Hall when you see him again in the summer. He will revel both in your prose and his own good judgement of your abilities. To wit: this is an excellent introduction:

Barbara Pym and the Church
by Felicity Halper

In 1980, when Barbara Pym died, little literary criticism had been written of her work. Five years later, the first of what was to become over twenty serious studies was published. All have been welcomed by the ever-expanding circle of Pym's readers. Some have found distinguished shelf space in libraries and universities. None have fully addressed the nucleus of religious sensibility in her work.

This year, three publishers on two continents will reprint seven separate Pym titles; universities in the United States and Canada will add her to their roster of writers worthy of their curricula; and the Barbara Pym Societies at Oxford and Harvard will attract distinguished scholars to their symposia. Barbara Pym has clearly emerged from her relative obscurity. Consequently, in an effort to 'place' her as a noteworthy literary figure, critics now compare her to Jane Austen, Anthony Trollope, Matthew Arnold, Charlotte M. Yonge, and Anita Brookner, among many others. Oddly, she shares some indefinable flavor with all of them. Yet she does not share the one characteristic that makes her work compelling in a contemporary context: Religion.

Religion (as opposed to spirituality), specifically the Church of England as redefined by The Oxford Movement, is at the heart of Pym's work. The circumscribed lives of her characters are universally shaped, centered, informed and curtailed by the Book of Common

161

Prayer, the horror of Rome, and the vestiges of a social order formed four hundred years before under the eye of a newly unified Church and State.

And I see you have read Tillyard. But I am going to stop here. This is too good to waste. If I comment on the whole essay, then you may not hand it in for your class. As it is, you must tell your Professor that I read the first page and thought it an excellent beginning. More than that you may not say, since. I can make no comment beyond this. Not now, anyway.

But I will for once, answer one of your personal questions.

Tomorrow.

Yours truly,

Mallory Cooper

Barbara Pym

January 23, 2_____

Dear Felicity,

You asked me why I have not written a book about Barbara Pym — and, that being the case, why Dr. Hall sent you to me to learn about her work.

Let me address this first by way of fact, then of history. I have, in fact, written a book on Barbara Pym. This is it.

As for history...

Perhaps it was the flu I had as a postgraduate — or simply the final seconds in a stage of the life cycle of any living thing — a child, a flower, a fruit, an idea — when the gestation is done and the new-formed thing manifests itself. But whatever it was, Lycidas, I now know, was its progenitor.

It has always seemed to me that Pym was not 'big enough' for me as you told me early in our acquaintance she was not for you. Why that was did not seem to be clear. Many scholars contentedly research the fragments of the obscure, the minor, the unfinished, the unknown, deep in the remote and dusty stacks of only the most specialised libraries, and no one thinks ill of it. It cannot be the oeuvre, therefore, that is wanting. Fifteen novels (published and unpublished) and twenty-seven short stories (not to mention unfinished material) constitute a substantial enough body of work.

Neither could it have been that the work itself was entirely unappreciated or even unexamined, although the latter term is relative with regard to the scope of most extant criticism. Pym's novels are, as I write, being reprinted and discussed in greater profusion than they have at any other time since she was born, largely thanks to the Internet.

Nor did it seem that this claim of 'not big enough' referred to, or sprang from, any fault inherent in the work — it just seemed that there was not enough for me (as opposed to a bona fide Pymophile) to do. I could enter neither the mild and decorous ranks of fandom, which might have produced a laudatory work, nor the earnest singular dedicated pursuit of the academician, which would eventuate in a conventional critical work.

Pym, as it were, could not be 'my man' in the way that the professors of my youth had 'men.' I could not say with complacent satisfaction or even composure of spirit 'I'm a Pym man', myself,' as they were wont to do. I remember those days of easy proclamation: 'I'm an Arnold (Milton, Wordsworth, Bacon, Donne, Hardy, etc.) man.'

The women expressed themselves differently of course — a step away. They were always 'researching' Woolf or Austen. They did not identify so internally with their work. As I suppose has always been the difference between the sexes.

But I was taught by these double-barrelled men and so felt constrained at least to be able to make some identifiable and identifying claim, even if unspoken. Yet, I could not. Thus, years having passed, I began re-reading Pym when I took up my doctoral studies, to find out why. After all, I had written acceptable academic work about other authors for my Bachelor's and Master's degrees — an originally absorbing journey that suddenly had little appeal. And there was value there — right there in the novels. I felt, but could not see it on every page.

And then I got the flu. Happily (for this purpose) it was severe enough to require heavy medication — the kind that at first dose absolves one from analytical thinking and later, with subsequent spoonfuls, any real thinking at all. What is left is a sort of diaphanous cognition — that elevated dream state that so often liberates truth from its captors by simply dissolving the tangle of scrutiny surrounding it. Something happened. Suddenly, having just that afternoon read Pym's unfinished work, *Civil to Strangers*, full of misapplied Wordsworthian quotations and 17th century exhortations, I remembered Lycidas. I also remembered three things:

1. What it was about Literature that I loved.
2. A short story on which I had just given a lecture to my students the week before. And (because my eye fell on the little notebook imprinted with the Mills College motto on the table beside me):
3. Who I really was.

In order these are:

1. The words themselves, which transcend all eras and fancies;
2. Isaac Asimov's short story, 'Profession', about a machine in the future that in one minute programs a child with the ability to read and later, when he is an adolescent with the knowledge to take up a profession and forever transforms his world; and
3. A writer.

I first came across Lycidas in the winter of 19___ when I was very young, very ignorant, and very much in love with the word and all its descendents. We were given Lycidas to read, to study, by that same professor who dumped our essays on Donne in the waste bin. Quite apart from the fact that I did not understand it, I loved it — its sound, its weight, its verbal finish. I did what I could to understand it and was pleased to discover a few facts — Virgil, Edward King — and a few new and fascinating words. I felt I knew more about it after this desultory research. Still, this bit of delving did not prepare me for what was to come when we went back into the classroom to discuss the poem: both a nightmare and a vision of heaven.

To make a very long story short, Dr. Terry took apart every line, every word and every thought we had about them — and threw the fragments at us like leaves in the wild west wind.

We had to examine the poem from within so to speak — to become by diligent pursuit, fully aware of every metaphor, and unfamiliar word, its history, its context, all classical reference, and all religious imagery and why they were employed. We then had to take this bright basket of definitions and facts back into the classroom where we (largely he) reconstructed the poem in all its glory, fully resonant with every nuance, and it shone on us like a Muse. I have never had so dramatic an example of how little words can mean and. one minute later, how much, when invested with a deep appreciation that can only be called love.

This is when I knew I didn't want to be a Milton-man, so to speak. I wanted to be Milton. Synecdochically, of course.

Like that child in the science fiction story I mentioned above, my literary life was transformed for me after that class. And now, I try to help transform it for others. This is why Dr. Hall and my other colleagues, when they come across a student with the same dissatisfactions, the same questions, the same inability to fit easily into the academy (and the same ability to succeed in it despite that) send him or her to me. You remember I tutor a fourteen-year-old university student. And others.

This is not to say that Milton and Barbara Pym are equivalent. They are not. But one meets Milton in Pym and can be led back to the Pierian Spring, and thus everywhere else. Everything is interrelated. This is how we have been looking at Barbara Pym. This is how I look at everything. This is why you have not, with all your dissatisfactions, abandoned your questions, your reading or this correspondence.

But then, this correspondence has never been about Barbara Pym, has it? It has been about you.

You did not object to silly men and mousy women because you don't want to *read* about characters such as these. You objected to them because you don't want to *write* about them. Your questions have always been personal — whether in reference to the novels or to me. You aren't really interested in reading *about* writing. You are interested in reading *for* writing. But you don't want to write about silly men and mousy women. (You have succeeded however in wanting to read about them. Well done.) You don't want to write like Barbara Pym.

Excellent!

To answer what I must insist be your last letter to me until your seminar is over, yes, my purpose was to illuminate literature for you the way it was illuminated for me. It was to encourage appreciative, practical, literary analysis, which is, I believe, an exercise and a talent far beyond current theory and criticism. But for you, unlike so many of your classmates, the analysis is not an end in itself. It is a beginning.

So you may answer your own original questions now, and because you can, I don't mind giving you my answer:

Why read literature and why read Barbara Pym?

So you can learn, Felicity, as boat-builders, butchers and dancers do, the profession for which you were meant.

You will be at ease now. You will find value in reading almost everything Barbara Pym wrote, now that you can approach her as a fellow writer — as an apprentice, perhaps, but a member of the profession all the same. This is why we study literature — to find out on which side of these pages we belong. Some will belong to those who respond to these pages and some will belong to those who create them. A few rare souls belong to both.

And so, now that you do not have to look through a critical lens that is not of your choosing, you will find pleasure in looking through all of them because you know that you need not employ any of them in your future life. They will be employed by future critics in the examination of your work, and you may accept or ignore them at will as you sit with your fellow writers in coffee houses (and on panels and with your readers) and talk about literature, not only because you once read *about* it but because you continue to read it, know it, love it and above all, create it. I hope you will not ignore all of these critics, for, among the labyrinths of nonsense, there is great, great worth. But that is for you to discover, in what I hope is opposition to me. Your literary history cannot be mine.

You asked me if I had any advice for you as you go back to university and begin your seminar on Barbara Pym.

No, Felicity. Not really. You already know that assumptions are destructive; that something is always happening when it appears not to be and that everything is part of something else. In the creation of one's future, that's about the best lesson anyone can learn.

Goodbye for now and good luck.

Mallory

PS And before you ask me what the motto of Mills College is, I will tell you so that you may take it into your classroom with you: 'Remember Who You Are and What You Represent.'

June 17, 2_____

Dear Felicity,

So. You received your grade. *Quod erat demonstrandum.* And yes, I am 'giving that address' at Yarmouth next Tuesday. Would you like to join me at the Faculty Club for tea at 4:00?

Very proud of you—

Mallory

Works Cited and/or Consulted

I hesitate to include a bibliography, lest the reader think this book is an attempt at a scholarly work. It is not. It began life as a creative (not scholarly) work for my MFA dissertation submitted in 1997 and was under a hundred pages, which is why many of the references below predate that publication date as indeed three quarters of this book predate others.

When I began to revise and augment Felicity and Barbara Pym *for trade publication, I simply expanded it without any further formal research, intending only to footnote quotations and references in order to give proper credit to other authors, and feeling, perhaps that re-researching would indicate that my own ideas were generated or supported by from works that had not yet been written when I finished my thesis. In fact, most of the quotations and allusions contained within it are those I remembered, wrote down, then went to check the source to see how accurate they were (or weren't).*

However, many works came to mind during the revision and while I did not study these books below, except those written by Barbara Pym, I did consult them. Mostly, however I just wrote the book from within the knowledge and education I already had and the hundreds of books I had already read — and then went back, purely out of interest, to see what others had to say about what I was thinking. At times what others had to say was so interesting that I went back to my manuscript and revised a paragraph or two — a page or two, in order to include it. And occasionally I was so interested in what another author had to say that I bought his or her book to read for pleasure after the first draft was submitted to Cinnamon Press.

This is not the way a work of literary criticism or any scholarly work is written. Thus, I trust that my original assertion that this is neither is fully supported by the paucity of references below.

Allen, Orphia Jane. *Barbara Pym: Writing a Life*. Metuchen: The Scarecrow Press, Inc., 1994.

Allen, Walter. *The English Novel*. Harmondsworth: Pelican, 1958.

Bailey, Adrian, *The Cooking of the British Isles*. New York: Time-Life Books, 1969.

Benet, Diana. *Something To Love*. Columbia: University of Missouri Press, 1986.

Budick, Sanford. *The Western Theory of Tradition: Terms and Paradigms of the Cultural Sublime.* New Haven: Yale University Press, 2000.

Burkhart, Charles. *The Pleasure of Miss Pym.* Austin: The University of Texas Press, 1987.

Butterworth, Eric, ed. *The Sociology of Modern Britain.* Glasgow: William Collins Sons & Co, 1974.

Cooper, Jilly. *Class.* London: Corgi Books, 1980.

Drabble, Margaret. *A Summer Bird-Cage.* Harmondsworth: Penguin Books, 1975.

Ellis, John M. *Literature Lost: Social Agendas and the Corruption of the Humanities.* New Haven: Yale University Press, 1997.

Empson, William. *Seven Types of Ambiguity.* Hammondsworth: Penguin Books, 1972.

Ford, Boris, ed. *The Pelican Guide to English Literature, Vols 1-7,* Hammondsworth: Penguin Books, 1969.

Forster, E. M. *Aspects of the Novel.* Harmondsworth: Pelican Books, 1962.

Fraser, G.S. *The Modern Writer and His World.* Harmondsworth: Penguin Books, 1967.

Fussell, Paul. *Class.* New York: Ballantine Books, 1984.

Frye, Northrop. *The Educated Imagination.* Bloomington: Indiana University Press, 1964.

Hazard, Paul. *Books, Children & Men.* The Horn Book, Inc., 1963.

Holt, Hazel and Pym, Hilary, eds. *A Very Private Eye.* New York: Dutton, 1984.

Holt, Hazel. *A Lot To Ask: A Life of Barbara Pym.* New York: Dutton, 1991.

James, Henry. *The Portrait of a Lady.* Harmondsworth: Penguin Books, 1970.

Kamuf, Peggy. *The Division of Literature or the University in Deconstruction.* Chicago: University of Chicago Press, 1997.

Kohr, Leopold. *The Academic Inn.* Aberystwyth: Y Lolfa Cyf, 1993.

Lamarque, Peter and Olsen, Stein Haugom. *Truth Fiction and Literature.* Oxford: Oxford University Press, 1994.

Leavis, F.R. *The Living Principle: 'English' as a Discipline of Thought.* Chicago: Elephant Paperbacks, 1998.

Liddell, Robert. *A Mind at Ease: Barbara Pym and Her Novels.* London: Peter Owen Publishers, 1989.

Little, Judy. *The Experimental Self: Dialogic Subjectivity in Woolf, Pym and Brooke-Rose.* Carbondale: Southern Illinois University Press, 1996.

Long, Robert Emmet. *Barbara Pym.* New York: The Ungar Publishing Company, 1986.

Maugham, W. Somerset. *Theatre.* Harmondsworth: Penguin Books, 1967.

Morley, David and Robins, Kevin, eds. *British Cultural Studies.* Oxford: Oxford University Press, 2001.

McCrum, Robert, Cran, William, and MacNeill, Robert. *The Story of English, Revised Edition.* New York: The Penguin Group, 1993.

Nardin, Jane. *Barbara Pym.* Boston: Twayne Publishers, 1985.

Mulhall, Stephen. *Wittgenstein's Private Language: Grammar, Nonsense, and Imagination in Philosophical Investigations, §§ 243-315.* Oxford: Oxford University Press, 2007.

Oliver, E. J. *Coventry Patmore.* New York: Sheed and Ward, 1956.

Patai, Daphne and Corral, Will H., eds. *Theory's Empire: An Anthology of Dissent.* New York: Columbia University Press, 2005.

Prose, Francine. *Reading Like a Writer: A Guide for People Who Love Books and For Those Who Want To Write Them.* New York: Harper Collins, 2006.

Pym, Barbara. *A Few Green Leaves.* New York: Dutton, 1980.

Pym, Barbara. *A Glass Of Blessings.* New York: Dutton, 1980.

Pym, Barbara. *An Academic Question.* New York: Dutton, 1986.

Pym, Barbara. *An Unsuitable Attachment.* New York: Dutton, 1982

Pym, Barbara. *Civil To Strangers and Other Writings.* New York: Dutton, 1987.

Pym, Barbara. *Crampton Hodnet.* New York: Dutton, 1985.

Pym, Barbara. *Excellent Women.* New York: New York: Dutton, 1978.

Pym, Barbara. *Jane and Prudence.* New York: Dutton, 1981.

Pym, Barbara. *Less Than Angels.* New York: Dutton, 1980.

Pym, Barbara. *No Fond Return Of Love.* New York: Dutton, 1982.

Pym, Barbara. *Quartet In Autumn.* New York: Dutton, 1978.

Pym, Barbara. *Some Tame Gazelle.* New York: Dutton, 1983.

Pym, Barbara. *The Sweet Dove Died.* New York: Dutton, 1979.

Raz, Orna. *Social Dimensions in the Novels of Barbara Pym, 1949-1963: The Writer as Hidden Observer.* New York: The Edwin Mellon Press, 2007.

Redlich, Monica. *Everyday England.* London: Gerald Duckworth & Co. Ltd., 1977.

Rossen, Janice. *Independent Women: The Function of Gender in the Novels of Barbara Pym.* New York: St Martin's Press, 1988.

Rossen, Janice. *The World of Barbara Pym.* New York: St. Martin's Press, 1987.

Shakespeare, William. *The Complete Plays and Poems of William Shakespeare.* eds. Neilson, William Allan, and Hill, Charles Jarvis. Cambridge: The Riverside Press, 1942.

Stevenson, Robert Louis. *A Child's Garden of Verses.* PD.

The Pick of Punch, 1958. (Bound excerpts. No other information given)

Thompson, Flora. *Lark Rise to Candleford.* Harmondsworth: Penguin Books, 1973.

Tillyard, M.M.W. *The Elizabethan World Picture.* Harmondsworth: Peregrine Books, 1963.

Tsagaris, Ellen M. *The Subversion of Romance in the Novels of Barbara Pym.* Bowling Green: Bowling Green State University Popular Press, 1998.

Turner, Victor W. and Bruner, Edward M. *The Anthropology of Experience.* Chicago: Univrsity of Illinois Press, 1986.

Weld, Annette. *Barbara Pym and the Novel of Manners.* New York, St. Martin's Press, 1992

West, Rebecca. *Harriet Hume.* New York: The Dial Press, 1980.

White, Antonia. *Frost in May.* London: Virago Ltd., 1978.

Witherspoon, Alexander M. and Warnke, Frank J. *Seventeenth Century Prose and Poetry.* New York: Harcourt, Brace & World, Inc., 1963.

Woolf, Virgina. *The Voyage Out.* London: Granada Publishing Ltd., 1977

Woolf, Virginia. *Three Guineas.* Harmondsworth: Penguin Books, 1977.

Zavaradeh, Mas'Ud. *The Mythopoeic Reality: The Postwar American Nonfiction Novel.* Chicago: University of Illinois Press, 1976.

Acknowledgements

I am grateful to those of my many academic colleagues who are also friends and who are not and never could be included in the general criticism of our profession contained in this book. Foremost among these are Dr. Ruth O. Saxton, Dean of Letters at Mills College, who supervised this text with meticulous attention when it was an MFA thesis and Dr. Thomas Strychacz, then Head of the English Department at Mills College, who was its earliest and most percipient reader. He thought Barbara Pym 'quite absurd' but applauded the manuscript anyway.

To Dr. William Marx, Reader, who had the unenviable task of supervising my doctoral thesis at the University of Wales and did it with great grace, for his unflagging solicitude not only in the preparation of that work, but also this one (and this author) throughout a very difficult time in the history of the institution, I am in profound and affectionate debt. I thank Professor John Manning originally at that same university (now at Purdue) who first saw in Barbara Pym great potential for a mixed-genre work such as this, written by an author such as I and said so supportively, robustly and often.

To dear Peter Miles, former Chair of the English Department also at that university, who read and loved every page of the original manuscript and wrote such a glowing account of it (which he slid under my office door one bleak winter afternoon) that I decided to actually finish it, I am profoundly grateful. I still carry his elegant appraisal in my briefcase.

To Beryl Doyle who helped immeasurably with a crucial part of my research and who can read between the lines better than anyone else: Diolch o galon i ti, a chariad mawr.

More seminally, my heartfelt thanks are due to Dr. Christopher J Terry, Examiner for Cambridge University (and former student of FR Leavis); my undergraduate advisor, my catalyst and my beloved friend, who over 30 years ago changed my relationship to the word and therefore literature forever.

I also have great pleasure in acknowledging the excellence of Dr. Jan Fortune-Wood, my editor and publisher at Cinnamon

Press. No one could have brought a better mind and heart to this work, or greater professionalism. Every encounter with Jan on this project has been warm, helpful and engaging.

In like manner, my thanks are due to Ann Drysdale whose meticulous editing and rich intellectual background made her the perfect guardian of this prose.

To two remarkably generous professionals, Laura Morris of The Laura Morris Literary Agency, who manages the Estate of Barbara Pym, and John McSpadyen of the Little, Brown Book Group, who is responsible for Permissions, I am deeply grateful for their 'randon acts of kindness' in the waiver of all fees for the quotations from Barbara Pym's novels that appear in this edition. I also thank Mr. McSpadyen for his equal generosity regarding the quotations from *Frost in May*.

Great thanks are due to the inestimable Hazel Holt, biographer and literary executor of Barbara Pym, not only for her magnanimous Foreword, her scrupulous inspection of my claims and postulations regarding Miss Pym (to which she gave full and unprecedented approval) but also for her charm, grace and serious attention to Toad in the Hole.

Russell Galen, my agent and friend of many years always has my deep appreciation, admiration and affection. He is a benison in my literary life, and his involvement with this book is gratefully acknowledged.

Special thanks are due to my kind friend and attorney, Harold Brown, Gang, Tyre, Ramer and Brown, Beverly Hills, California, for his inestimable advice and assiduity regarding certain matters attendant on the text of this book

To William McClung, former editor at the University of California Press, a very dear friend, I owe a singular debt of gratitude — for the constancy of his support, his intelligent advocacy and his catalytic inspiration in my early literary endeavours, and for the Good Table, but above all, for his innate chivalry, natural kindness and grand civility in a mad, mad world.

To my family goes my deepest gratitude: my parents for their unfailing love and generosity and for providing a secluded place in which to finish the last stages of this manuscript; my sons, Christopher and Richard for their incomparable devotion, perspicacity and munificence; my stepdaughter, Jody, for her warmth, enthusiasm and keen editorial eye; my daughters-in-law Amelie and Jodi for their countless thoughtful acts during the writing of this book.

Above all, I thank my husband, partner and best friend, Herb, without whom was made nothing that has been made, whose love is above description, whose magnanimity knows no limit and whose great gifts to me have often included parts of myself.